Symbolic structures
An exploration of the culture of the Dowayos

This book is published as part of the joint publishing agreement established in 1977 between the Fondation de la Maison des Sciences de l'Homme and the Press Syndicate of the University of Cambridge. Titles published under this arrangement may appear in any European language or, in the case of volumes of collected essays, in several languages.

New books will appear either as individual titles or in one of the series which the Maison des Sciences de l'Homme and the Cambridge University Press have jointly agreed to publish. All books published jointly by the Maison des Sciences de l'Homme and the Cambridge University Press will be distributed by the Press throughout the world.

Cet ouvrage est publié dans le cadre de l'accord de co-édition passé en 1977 entre la Fondation de la Maison des Sciences de l'Homme et le Press Syndicate of the University of Cambridge. Toutes les langues européennes sont admises pour les titres couverts par cet accord, et les ouvrages collectifs peuvent paraître en plusieurs langues.

Les ouvrages paraissent soit isolément, soit dans l'une des séries que la Maison des Sciences de l'Homme et Cambridge University Press ont convenu de publier ensemble. La distribution dans le monde entier des titres ainsi publiés conjointement par les deux établissements est assurée par Cambridge University Press.

Symbolic structures

An exploration of the culture of the Dowayos

Nigel Barley

Assistant Keeper, Museum of Mankind
(the Ethnography Department of the British Museum)

Cambridge University Press

Cambridge
London   New York   New Rochelle   Melbourne   Sydney

& Editions de la Maison des Sciences de l'Homme
Paris

CAMBRIDGE UNIVERSITY PRESS
Cambridge, New York, Melbourne, Madrid, Cape Town, Singapore, São Paulo, Delhi

Cambridge University Press
The Edinburgh Building, Cambridge CB2 8RU, UK

With Editions de la Maison des Sciences de l'Homme
54 Boulevard Raspail, 75270 Paris Cedex 06, France

Published in the United States of America by Cambridge University Press, New York

www.cambridge.org
Information on this title: www.cambridge.org/9780521105347

First published 1983
This digitally printed version 2009

A catalogue record for this publication is available from the British Library

Library of Congress Catalogue Card Number: 82-23651

ISBN 978-0-521-24745-0 hardback
ISBN 978-0-521-10534-7 paperback

Contents

Acknowledgments

Field research was conducted in northern Cameroon from June 1977 to September 1978 and from April 1979 to August 1979. It was funded by the Social Science Research Council to whom thanks are due. The Dowayos were first brought to my attention by Phil Burnham of University College London who was a very present help in many difficulties thereafter. A special vote of thanks must go to the Sudan Mission of Ngaoundere, without whose aid this research could never have been completed; to Ron Nelson who made available his Dowayo material and experience; to Jim Noss who rescued my finances; to the Blues for hospitality and to all for their generosity and good fellowship. Elizabeth and Marinus Wiering introduced me to the Dowayo language: I thank them for their unstinted help and apologise that the linguistic material here falls short of their own high standards. Fieldwork permission was granted by the Office Nationale de Recherches Scientifiques et Techniques (ONAREST), Cameroon. I gratefully acknowledge the help of the sous-préfet of Poli in making official files available to me. Most of all, I thank the alumni of the Fort Berg Field Research Station for aid and encouragement, sanctuary and supplies, conversation and medication. A special acknowledgment goes to Barney.

Parts of this work were presented in embryonic form at seminars in University College London and the Museum of Mankind. Discussions with Mike and Joanna Kaplan have been an especially rich source.

Preface

It is a hot, sticky day even by West African standards. A mid-afternoon drowsiness hangs over the hillside village. At one side of a small dusty compound a group of men are crouched, giggling and joking as they work. Before them stands a spherical water-jar that they are decorating with strips of cloth, horsetails and strange, metal objects. It is clear that the men have been drinking. At one stage, they have broken off their work and demanded more drink before consenting to continue.

Over the other side of the compound, a white man, an anthropologist, is slumped in the shade, notebook and camera abandoned beside him. He is haggard, having just suffered a bad bout of malaria. His hands tremble with incipient hepatitis. He sweats profusely and tries to keep his befogged mind on the events taking place before him. Slightly to one side, is another white man, a dentist, an American fresh from the United States. He glows with health and alert interest. He is simply visiting the area for the day, making a brief excursion from the world of mission bungalows and international hotels to see life in the bush for himself. He turns to the anthropologist and smiles endearingly. 'Why are they doing this?' he asks politely. 'What does the jar mean?'

The anthropologist begins to mutter an interpretation. Each explanatory statement seems to demand four more to justify and interpret the one before. The dentist looks puzzled and disappointed. The anthropologist feels he is letting down his audience and betraying his art. He tries harder. Before he knows where he is, he is giving an introductory lecture on symbolic interpretation. The dentist looks more puzzled, then bored. His attention wanders and he begins to examine the state of the men's teeth as they joke with each other. The anthropologist detects the loss of attention and promises to write to his companion, explaining the whole thing better. This book is the result of that promise.

My dentist had had the benefit of some introductory courses in anthropology, which is doubtless why he assumed in the first place that the jar 'meant' something. The 'meaning' of the jar is the problem about which this work will revolve.

In a work of anthropology, it is customary to begin with some sort of a description of the general ethnographic background. This serves the useful purpose of locating the people firmly in space and time and separating them from the undifferentiated mass of 'primitive man'. Whatever the virtues for the reader of such an approach, for the writer it is a valuable device, conveying in a small space what would otherwise have to be introduced piecemeal throughout the work in the form of footnotes, unnecessarily impeding the flow and clogging the analysis.

At the end of this work, I append a detailed description of a number of important Dowayo festivals that have been treated in the text. This admittedly constitutes a somewhat indigestible whole but will be appreciated by the serious student who will wish to check analyses for himself. I have made this section as full as was possible. One of the major failings of current work on symbolic studies is partiality. What it cannot incorporate in its description, it simply fails to notice. It is hoped that this section will allow students to judge for themselves to what degree the lowest levels of descriptive adequacy have been achieved and perhaps to improve the work by their own contributions.

The language of the Dowayo people, which for reasons of simplicity I shall term Dowayo, is tonal.[1] It has four static tones that can be combined to form glides. The depiction of these in the orthography is a complex and costly business and at the moment of writing no final decision has been made between ONAREST in Cameroon and the Summer Institute of Linguistics (which has conducted research into the language under the direction of Elizabeth and Marinus Wiering) as to what orthographic system should be adopted. I have therefore found it expedient to omit marking of tones as these can have no value for those unfluent in the tongue and may be easily inferred by those few who are. Again, for reasons of general convenience, I mark the change from open to closed vowel by the addition of *h* (i.e. *e* is the vowel of Fr. *elle*, while *eh* is the final vowel of Fr. *aimé*). Crossing of consonants indicates glottalisation; tilde over a word indicates nasalisation.

A number of diagrams are used in the course of the work. An attempt has been made to develop each from those that precede it, so that they constitute one of the principal sources of continuity.

1 The ethnographic background

The Dowayos are a pagan, montagnard people numbering some fifteen thousand and living in the Poli region of north Cameroon, West Africa, close to the Nigerian border (see fig. 1). Hitherto, they have been largely grouped together with other pagans of that area – such tribes as the Koma, Bata, Pape (Dupa) and Ninga – under the general term *Kirdi* or the highly pejorative *Namchi*. Even the French colonial administration was unable to fix on a firm division of these peoples between Poli and the Nigerian frontier, and many of the works purportedly dealing with the Dowayos deal instead with the Koma or the Pape, or cannot be definitely assigned to the ethnography of any one single group.[2]

The area is dominated by the Fulani. Sedentary Fulani run the cities and major towns throughout the north, while nomadic Fulani claim rights of passage in the dry season when they come down in search of grazing. Poli is regarded by Dowayos as a blatant Fulani incursion into their territory. The various groups define themselves, above all, in opposition to the Islamic Fulani, who regarded the whole area as a hunting reserve for domestic slaves and levied various forms of tribute until recent times.

The Dowayos themselves have a very firm notion of who they are and disclaim all kinship with surrounding peoples. They divide themselves into two groups, mountain Dowayos (*Tēehreh*) and plains Dowayos (*Markeh*). These terms are self-explanatory to a certain degree but there exists the feeling that mountain Dowayos are more traditional and hold to the old ways better, that they are more truly Dowayo. With the mountain Dowayos, it is sometimes important to distinguish between those of the eastern Mango and those of the western Godet ranges. While the rainchiefs live in the east, the principal 'Masters of the Earth', whose job it is to maintain the fertility of the fields, centre on Daksidongo in the west. These distinctions will become clearer in the course of the analysis. It may be mentioned here that there is no justification whatever for Lembezat's assertions that the 'Master of the Earth' is of Bata origin and that the rainchief is a Pape (Lembezat 1961: 175). Possibly confusion has crept in from the use of Bata and Pape (Dupa) songs and ritual artefacts in Dowayo

1

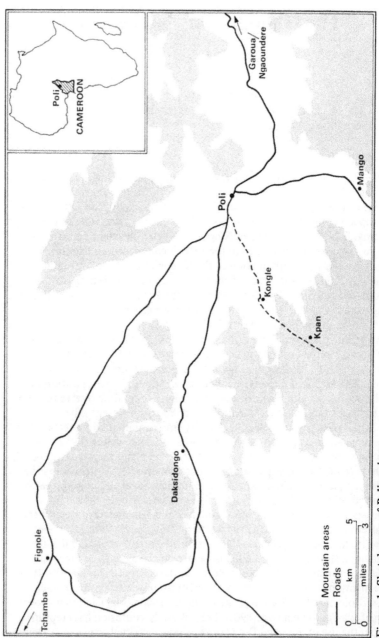

Figure 1 Sketch map of Poli region

ceremonial. I made a special point of checking that they both hold themselves to be, and are considered by others as, true Dowayos.

The Dowayos have no clear tradition of origin. When questioned on the subject, in typical Dowayo fashion they merely reply that they are where they have always been, where they belong. Efforts by previous scholars to assign a northeastern origin to the Dowayos derive either from the conviction that all current conditions are to be explained by the Fulani expansion of the nineteenth century or simply from the belief that all Kirdi must have a common origin. Given the impossibility of clearly identifying the tribes mentioned by early travellers, it is unclear to what period one should assign the occupation of the mountains by the Dowayos. It seems likely that it is not to be entirely dissociated from the occupation of the area by the Fulani in the course of the nineteenth century, Fulani cavalry being useless in the granite outcrops of the highlands. This must have led to at least a concentration of Dowayos in the mountains. French administrative policy, on the other hand, sought to reverse this process by encouraging the Dowayos to descend from the arid Godet range and settle in the surrounding plains. This has resulted in many plains-dwelling Dowayos having traditional links of kinship and skull-house affiliation with mountain Dowayos. Thus, some Dowayos, though long resident in the plains, still maintain that they are mountain Dowayos and may retain the name of their highland village so that there are two Dowayo villages with the same name. Like many other Dowayo categories, that of mountain Dowayo is prescriptive, rather than a descriptive term.

Dowayos are acephalous, although chiefs were introduced by the French. These, however, are totally lacking in power and authority, being scorned by traditional Dowayos who resent their interference, and largely ignored by modernistic youth who regard them as an anachronism in the world of national politics.

The term *waaryo* 'chief' denotes a much more fundamental Dowayo distinction between a rich man (who owns cattle) and a poor one (who does not). This distinction constantly recurs in Dowayo life. Only rich men can organise the major festivals at which cattle must be killed. Only rich men can help with marriage payments. In theory this should allow the development of all forms of patronage and clientship. Land is abundant and it is only shortage of labour that limits a man's production of millet. In fact, patronage is embryonic, being reserved almost exclusively for the blacksmith. Nowadays, poor men seek cash labour in the cities to raise money to begin a herd. Previously, I was told, the only alternative was to act as herdsman for a rich man. After a certain number of years, the man would be rewarded with a female calf.

Normally, residence is patrilocal. A mature man will have his own hut and granary within a circular, enclosing palisade that also contains the compounds of his wives. Polygyny is frequent amongst rich men, three wives being about average, though men of special wealth such as cantonment chiefs or rainmakers may have twelve or thirteen. A typical compound is illustrated in fig. 2. Compounds are not aligned in any particular geographical direction but according to local exigencies. Highland Dowayo villages are arranged to form 'streets' with roofs of huts in different compounds almost touching. Approach paths are deliberately made circuitous and difficult for reasons of security. Entry is either via a stile or through a low hut that must be wriggled through on one's belly.

Generally, a man will dwell with close patrilineal kinsmen whose compounds will be those adjacent to his own and clustered around the cattle-park where the communally owned cattle are kept at night. Physical distance correlates approximately with kinship distance, collateral kinsmen being at some small remove while herding in common. Always apart is the blacksmith, with his women, the potters, preferably divided from the rest of the village by a stretch of uncleared bush or a road. Once again, spatial distance is here a measure of social distance. Blacksmiths, as we shall see later, are endogamous, endophagous and require a separate water supply.

While patrilineal links tie together co-residents, the major functioning social unit is the skull-house group. This is called into play for the organisation of festivals and the diagnosis and treatment of disease. Communality of herding and skull-house membership are far from being conterminous. Several herding arrangements are normally associated with a single skull-house and clear kinship links between all members of the same skull-house will not often be traceable. Moreover, members of several skull-houses will occasionally decide, for reasons of mutual convenience, to herd together. Nevertheless, it is the case that skull-house membership passes from father to children of both sexes. A woman retains membership of her father's skull-house throughout marriage. The role of these groupings in organising rituals will be treated later.

Despite the emphasis on patrilineal kinship, terminology is basically ego-centred and cognatic (see fig. 3). Outside the nuclear family, it is striking for the degree to which it carries through the principle of reciprocity. If A employs a given term for B, then B uses the same for A. This seems to be the fundamental structural principle of the terminology. Marriage with any named relative is not permitted. Young people are expected to be sexually active from about the age of eight years and a mother will readily permit a boy to spend the night with her daughter in the girl's hut in her compound. When the mother sleeps with her husband this normally occurs in the husband's sleeping hut, according to a rigorously enforced rota agreed between co-wives. Should a boy wish to take a girl as wife, negotiations concerning brideprice must be opened by an intermediary. The price must include cattle, preferably a breeding pair,

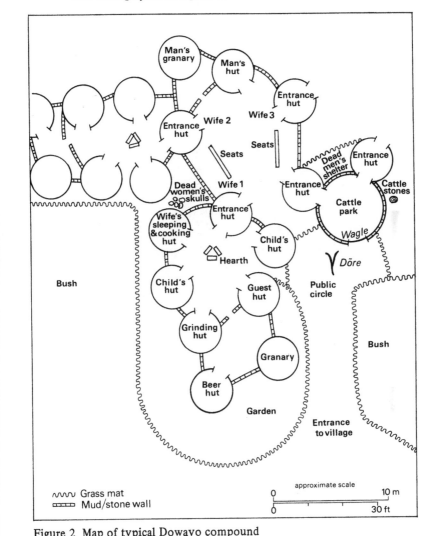

Figure 2 Map of typical Dowayo compound

6

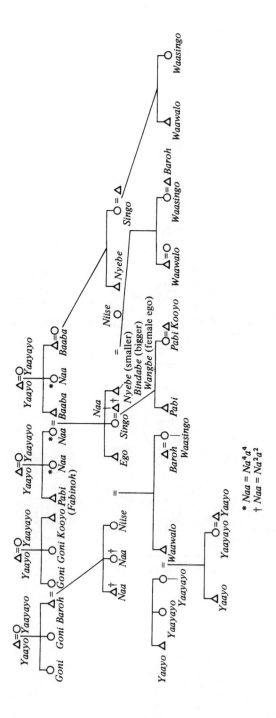

Figure 3

and the balance will be made up with lesser livestock (sheep and goats), robes, and the thick cotton cloth the Dowayos weave to wrap their dead in. There is no marriage ceremony. The couple are considered wed when the woman moves to the man's village, as opposed to his coming to spend the night with her. Children of either sex belong to the husband's group. Divorce is frequent, it being rare to meet a Dowayo of any age who does not have at least one terminated marriage to her credit. Normally, the wife simply runs away from her husband or he will inform his wife's father that he no longer requires her as wife. In theory, the brideprice is then refunded, but all Dowayos know that the chances of a complete reimbursement are small and have already hedged their bets by delaying full payment as long as possible. Thus marriage is a somewhat fluid arrangement, with many on their way into it or out of it at any one time. Any one woman will simultaneously occupy several different places in the system.

Should the bride die in the first year of marriage, a man will try to oblige his wife's kin to make another woman available, though they will resist this and seek to invoke the *caveat emptor* principle that obtains in the wider sphere of trade relations. On a man's death, his wives may be inherited by his brothers or adult sons, by mutual consent. A son may not, of course, inherit his true mother. Alternatively, a widow may return to her native village with some part of the brideprice refunded. If she is an old woman this may be waived. Even this is a cause of much litigation. It cannot be overstressed that brideprice disputes are the chief source of social disruption in Dowayo village life.

Dowayos engage in subsistence agriculture, the basic crop being millet. Various yams, peanuts, gombo, taro, beans, melons and peppers are also grown in smaller quantities. The only cash crop is cotton, grown under strong government pressure; and some rice is produced under the direction of missionaries. In the Godet range, there are numerous borassus palms, not found in any number elsewhere in Dowayoland. In the Mango range, plentiful year-round water from the high mountains permits irrigation in the dry season that extends from about October to April. Men and women engage in agriculture equally. A man may cultivate jointly with his wife but more often they will have separate fields and always separate granaries. Men who specialise in agriculture – 'true cultivators' (*baakyaayo*) – constitute a special class. Sowing occurs about the beginning of April, when the first small rains have fallen. From about June, Dowayos take up semi-permanent residence in small woven huts in their fields; and a series of hoeing parties is held, beer being given in exchange for labour. The harvest occurs in late November, just after the establishment of the dry season. Except in the small area where irrigation is practised, no cultivation occurs between November and April. The women make baskets, fish with poison and dams, and go on visits to relatives. The men hunt, fish with line and spear and hold various of the lesser festivals. Increasingly, there is a tendency for young men to leave after the harvest to seek wage labour in the cities of Garoua and Ngaoundere. Most return next year in time for planting.

Cattle are the major value in Dowayo life and the principal obstacle to successful agriculture. They are allowed to wander promiscuously across the fields and inflict great damage on the crops. In theory, at night they should be returned to the central cattle park but this is often allowed to lapse. During the growing season, Dowayos may often be encountered, crouched weeping in the ruins of their fields, comforting themselves with the knowledge that their cattle have committed similar acts in the fields of their neighbours. In former times, boys were required to look after the cattle and guard the fields. Nowadays compulsory school removes them from these tasks and children are, moreover, treated with a generous indulgence that frees them from almost all parental discipline. They devote themselves to the unfettered play of their imaginations and all manner of mischief, and are hardly ever punished by their doting parents. Cattle are rarely sold. Traditionally, they were killed only for the dead during funerals and skull-festivals and most meat is still acquired according to rules of distribution to kin on such occasions.

Specialist offices such as circumciser, sorcerer, clown and healer exist but political decisions are made at the hamlet level by the meeting of all mature men. Elders speak with special authority, but there is no way of enforcing a decision in the face of dissent. Very often lawsuits will simply die on their feet after lengthy litigation since the parties cannot be obliged to appear or because no mutually acceptable compromise can be reached. Dowayos behave with an unquestioned disdain for external involvement in their affairs and avoid sending cases to the local court in Poli. They fear the agents of the central government and use magical remedies to keep them away, regarding them as simply another form of misfortune. This attitude has won them a reputation in the outside world as stubborn and uncooperative.

Dowayoland is still very much a closed area. Communications are appalling, bridges are frequently washed down and roads are impassable. The Dowayos have very little to do with the wider commercial world dominated by their traditional enemies, the Fulani. They dislike buying and selling, though the younger men and women covet radios, bicycles and Western clothes. They disapprove strongly of the poll-tax which obliges them to use money. 'If it was not for taxation,' I was told, 'you would not see money among the Dowayos.' The payment of brideprice in money is thus totally unacceptable. Fathers know that money disappears among fellow kinsmen whereas cattle multiply. It seems that in former times, burial cloth, cattle and hoe-blades were the media of exchange, with various restrictions on the direction of these commodities between affines. The precise articulation of this system can now only be guessed at.

Of fundamental importance in Dowayo life are a number of rites of passage. Whereas birth and marriage are not matters of great ceremonial, circumcision of boys and death are the subject of great ritual elaboration. After death, a man's skull and a woman's water-jar are the objects of further ceremonies which will be the subject of later analysis. I describe these in detail in the appendix.

Also to be noted is the pervasive Dowayo attitude to the Fulani, their traditional masters and — as noted — enemies. Old men, especially, react to the mention of Fulani with powerful emotions of hatred and scorn. This, however, is tinged with grudging admiration. The Fulani, after all, are rich and powerful. They have even displaced the White Man, a process that baffles Dowayos. The French clearly encouraged the Dowayos to Fulanicise themselves.[3] Whereas the young often opt for Christian modernism as a way of bettering their lot, older Dowayos deck themselves with the trappings of Fulani chieftains as a claim to status. Rich men wear Fulani robes and swords, carry red umbrellas, etc. All this, as will be shown, goes with the notion that most of the attributes of culture are importations from surrounding peoples, especially from the Fulani who gave them the most vital attribute of their civilisation — circumcision.

2   Symbolism and the punctuation of culture

The word 'symbolism' has come to be used in such a variety of senses that it no longer constitutes a well-defined category. It has been used as an etic category of the observer, an emic category used by the observed, a discrete class of behaviour, and an aspect of all behaviour. The simplest and most pervasive viewpoint in anthropology can be summed up as: 'This looks crazy. It must be symbolism.'

Such a tendency is to be found in Sperber's (1974: 4) criterion of symbolicity, once it has been stripped of elegant expression. Thus, he writes: 'I note then as symbolic all activity where the means put into play [sic] seem to me to be clearly disproportionate to the explicit or implicit end, whether this end be knowledge, communication or production – that is to say all activity whose rationale escapes me.' The tradition is one sanctioned by generations of anthropological practice. The decision to interpret behaviour as 'symbolic' is often the product of the failure of the anthropologist to comprehend something, plus a dogmatic commitment to the rationality of primitive man. The result is as uneasy as the literary critic who blandly regards poetry as merely deviant language. The normal becomes thereby firmly cut off from symbolic analysis. As Sperber remarks concerning Dorze food: 'When a Dorze eats a normally buttered dish, no symbolism need be postulated . . . In other words, an element takes on its symbolic value to the extent that it departs from a norm' (1974: 61).

In this way, two categories disappear from ethnographic accounts. The first is that of 'nonsense' since primitive man is always sensible (in functional analysis) or at least rational (though this term defies clear analysis).[4] The second casualty is that of the cultural classifications that define normality within a given culture. Thus, in the case of food classifications alluded to above, the normal structure of Dorze ethnocuisine is resubmerged in the morass of 'ethnographic background' as if Levi-Strauss (1964), Leach (1964), Tambiah (1969) and Douglas (1975) had never written. By now, many well-documented cases have been examined, going back at least to Needham (1962), showing how aspects of culture that

10

would otherwise be assigned to disparate areas of study such as economics, kinship, politics and symbolism can be articulated according to a single structural form. It is this literature that supports structuralism's major claim to be interesting and important rather than a mere epiphenomenon of no general applicability.

In fact, Sperber's definition of his own criterion of symbolicity is inadequate to define his own usage. Symbolism is not merely irrationality. Symbolicity is irrationality plus an explanation. Putting butter on one's head among the Dorze is not symbolic merely because it 'looks crazy'. It is symbolic because Sperber can produce an explanation that fits it into a wider scheme of things by subjecting it to the various processes that we have come to recognise as symbolic. Thus, analyses such as those of Needham (1962) are not symbolic merely because they deal with some seemingly baffling and irrational material. They go beyond this to show how very basic structuring principles can point out order where all seemed chaos. All such analyses rest ultimately on Levi-Strauss's fundamental insight into the nature of cultural forms and the transformational processes that allow one structure to be mapped from one area to another.

In these terms, it now becomes very difficult to justify a distinction between 'rational' and 'irrational' areas of culture since both may rest upon the same basic structures that define reality – a world-view that few would wish to deny the appellation 'symbolic'. At the same time, the latter differ intuitively from the former in that we call into play, in their interpretation, secondary processes that we also term 'symbolic'.

The chief of these is perhaps representational symbolism of the 'A represents/symbolises/"is" B' sort, but there are many others, e.g. structural models involving transformation, models involving connotation and communication, rhetorical models. We shall look at some of these in connection with concrete examples later in this book and sometimes have to consider the relative merits of different models applied to the same case.

Many of these interpretative processes are derived from linguistic models which have constituted something of an area of growth over recent years. One might sum up the change from structural-functionalism to contemporary anthropology as a switch from a model of 'discourse as action' to 'action as discourse'.

It will be appreciated that the effect of this is greatly to enlarge the area of culture to which 'symbolic' interpretations are applied. In the process, formal models, deriving as they do from linguistics, may suffer severe 'stretching'. Foremost among the casualties is the term 'meaning', followed closely by 'communication'. It is an assumption of much that follows that to show that an area has structure is not to show that it has meaning or communicates something. Moreover, it leaves the basic anthropological problem of rationality unresolved, indeed untouched. In the apparent dilemma between a functionalist approach to ritual that treats it in terms of its effects and a crudely representational interpretation that regards it as 'about' something else, structuralism offers a third way out. This will become clearer in the course of the analysis.

If we accept that a world-view is in every sense as 'symbolic' as the interpretative processes that also bear that name, then the first concern of the cultural anthropologist is to map out some of the basic structures that give it form. I shall therefore begin with a description of the ways in which Dowayo culture is punctuated and divided into spheres and domains. In later sections, I shall have to deal with more complex structures and devices, considering at some length some of the rituals of Dowayo culture. This is not because the symbolic is held to be synonymous with the irrational and non-pragmatic but simply because these offer a closed group in Dowayo culture, a privileged hunting-ground for those structures to be found in all parts of their social formations.

The first significant distinction made by Dowayos is between ordinary Dowayo and blacksmith.[5] Blacksmiths, as mentioned, form an endogamous caste. Its male members make the tools of war, agriculture and circumcision. Its female members are the potters who make the implements of cooking and brewing. Although the restrictions on blacksmiths have been significantly relaxed under the influence of missionaries and other outside contacts, they are still vigorously enforced outside the immediate Godet area especially around Mango where the main rainchiefs live. In everyday speech, Dowayos often distinguish between 'Dowayos' and 'blacksmiths' as if they constitute two entirely separate categories. The opposition between the two is marked in a number of ways. Ordinary Dowayos may not copulate with blacksmiths, nor eat from the same vessel. Blacksmiths should not enter a man's compound and never a woman's. Their women may not draw water where other Dowayo women do, being obliged to use their own source of water or be served by another. Although Dowayos regularly share cigarettes, no one would do so with a blacksmith. Food may be accepted from a blacksmith only if it afterwards undergoes some cultural process such as cooking (or shelling in the case of peanuts). A blacksmith will normally be the client of a chief to whom he is obliged to give his services free in return for help in marriage payments. Many blacksmiths, moreover, are prevented from owning cattle by their 'hot hands' — the result of excessive contact with fire — which would kill livestock. In such a situation a chief acts as banker for them, giving and receiving marriage payments on their behalf. By the standards of the culture, blacksmiths are very wealthy but 'dirty' (*dtibto*). We will recognise the familiar phenomenon of an opposition between blacksmith and ordinary Dowayo being reflected in controls on communication across several domains — food, sex, physical space. Various other data are ordered by such an opposition. When a steer is killed, the blacksmith takes the anus and large intestine; some will even eat the vagina, a fact that other Dowayos greet with horror. There is a general belief that blacksmiths eat dogs, though I never found one who would admit to it. On one unfortunate occasion, a decision was made to slaughter a sterile cow to repay an outstanding debt of meat. When the beast was disembowelled, the foetus of a calf was found inside. There was much discussion as to whether this was edible. In the end it was assigned to the blacksmith as his part.

The blacksmith does not belong to the same skull-house as his patron. Blacksmiths belong to separate skull-houses with no ordinary Dowayo members. At a skull-festival, when a rich man has organised the dance with the skulls of his ancestors, the blacksmith's skulls are kept to one side initially and removed from the pile again at the end.

Assuming, then, an opposition between these two classes of Dowayo, we see that it is important to subdivide further the class of blacksmith in a manner showing all the characteristics we have some to expect of the binary contrast. We must note the distinction between male and female. The female blacksmith has the monopoly on pottery but also a second skill of which, although not the exclusive practitioner, she is the acknowledged expert — midwifery. Her husband, on the other hand, was formerly executioner and handler of the dead.[6] One brought Dowayos into the world, the other sent them from it (see fig. 4).

There is one further mark of the separateness of the blacksmith, a disease which other Dowayos may incur from excessive contact with them. Since, however, this involves structures more complex than that of the simple binary split, I shall deal with this elsewhere.

Mention has already been made of the rainmaker. He, too, has a special place in the scheme of things. There are two principal rainmakers in Dowayoland, both in the Mango range, and thus mountain Dowayos. In everyday speech the term *gāatyaayo* 'mountain man' is used as the

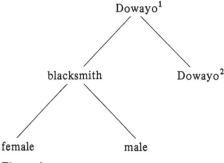

Figure 4

standard word for a man with these powers. Ordinary Dowayos visiting the Mango area may not draw water for themselves. The arm that draws the water will be afflicted by an eruption of boils. Dowayos must be offered water by 'mountain men', just as they offer it to blacksmiths, and I have often seen them suffer real distress during treks in the hot season, going all day without drink rather than break this prohibition. Also, 'mountain men' on visits in other areas of Dowayoland have to exercise great care when eating and drinking. It is explained that they have strengthened themselves with special 'roots'[7] for their mystical functions and would go blind if they consumed sesame. In consequence sesame is forbidden to them although consumed elsewhere in Dowayoland. It would even be dangerous to eat from a dish that had previously contained sesame. Ordinary Dowayos are dangerous to them and they must exercise great care. They, on the other hand, are viewed with deep suspicion by other Dowayos. Mountain Dowayos suffer from goitre and are supposed deliberately to communicate the disease to plains Dowayos by rubbing yams against the swellings and selling them at the market. Mountain Dowayos are known to be able to afflict plains Dowayos with drought or strike them down with lightning if they feel that hospitality is insufficient. Instead of Dowayo women being unavailable to them, they are notorious for the way in which they freely take them without payment. The Old Man of Kpan, chief rainmaker, has some thirteen wives and boasts not to have paid brideprice for any. We can depict this as in fig. 5.

But there is more to this. Relations between rainchief and blacksmith are clearly marked by a stronger opposition than the other two terms. Blacksmiths are even banned from rainmakers' villages. Should they inadvertently enter one, the rainchief would die from a cough. Should a rainchief walk through a village where a blacksmith is firing pots, they would all burst. Relations are polarised between rainchief and blacksmith with ordinary Dowayos as a middle term (fig. 6).

The women of rainchiefs can be given to any ordinary Dowayo (though not to a blacksmith) provided he allows his spouse to replace all cooking pots that may have been polluted by sesame and ensures that she never drinks water that contains unmediated rainfall. In effect, this means that a

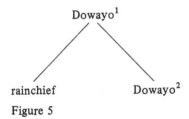

Figure 5

'mountain man's' daughter must always cook inside and never leave water-jars uncovered. Given the other restrictions on water and food exchange obtaining amongst the Dowayos, we can depict relations in the form of an analogue gradient as in fig. 7. We shall have to return to the subject of water at a later stage (p. 50).

A similarly tripartite schema underlies the natural world of animate beings. Humans and animals are assigned to different domains which are variously related.

Looking first at humans (*doohde*), it is important to note native ideas of conception. The woman is viewed after the classic model whereby she is a vessel in which the man deposits his seed. This merges with menstrual blood to form the child which is nourished by the woman's body till birth. Conception consists of stopping menstrual flow. The man, however, must continue to have regular intercourse with the woman during pregnancy in order to 'form' the child. Adultery by a woman after conception would result in miscarriage ('the water would go away'). At a more abstract level, Dowayos explain that conception is caused by a spirit entering the womb. This may be the ancestral spirit (*looreyo*) of a lineal ancestor of either partner which is then reincarnated in the child. It is normally not possible to identify which particular ancestor is involved, nor do Dowayos accept the implication that such a system placed a theoretical upper limit on their numbers. These beliefs serve to explain why intercourse may occur without conception and the observed facts of resemblances between parents and children.

The spirits of ancestors are thought to inhere in the skulls which are

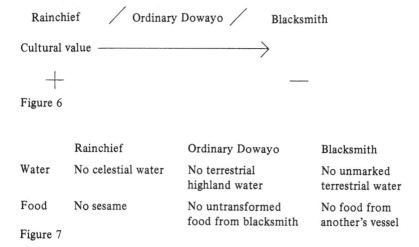

Rainchief   / Ordinary Dowayo /   Blacksmith

Cultural value ——————————————→

＋   —

Figure 6

	Rainchief	Ordinary Dowayo	Blacksmith
Water	No celestial water	No terrestrial highland water	No unmarked terrestrial water
Food	No sesame	No untransformed food from blacksmith	No food from another's vessel

Figure 7

removed after death and undergo complex treatment before being placed, in the case of males, in a skull-house far out in the bush, or in the case of women, stored under a tree in a similarly remote position. Ancestors are held to be capricious and dangerous, irritable and spiteful. Relations with them must be carefully regulated and women are especially prone to harassment from dead relatives who will refuse to make them pregnant. If divination reveals that the spirit of a particular relative is responsible for this infertility, offerings of beer, blood or excrement will be made on the skull.

The male skull-house, which takes the form of an ordinary Dowayo hut, and its immediate environs are completely forbidden to women who would anger the spirits with their smell and become sterile as a result. Female skulls are also held to be dangerous to women, though less immediately so than male ones.

The animal sphere is divided into 'beasts of the village' (*namraatumyo*) and 'beasts of the bush' (*namhētumyo*). 'Beasts of the village' are the Dowayo dwarf cattle, sheep, goats and chickens. The fertility of cattle is assured by certain stones (*nasāale*) (fig. 8) which are buried in a pot beside the cattle-park of a rich man. They are offered blood, cattle-excrement or beer when cattle are slain. They are in some sense 'alive' and move. A

Figure 8

woman should not pass near them, lest they make her sterile. A man should approach them with care lest his testicles swell up. A man with the smell of adultery on him might cause them to disappear into the bush entirely. For these reasons, the stones are handled by old men whose procreative powers are on the wane. Owners say that they were given to them by the ancestors and cannot be divided. The impossibility of keeping cattle without access to these stones is one of the major arguments used against the splitting of the herd.

Similar stones ensure the reproduction of the other domestic animals — goat-stones, for example, are buried under their shelter. Only the cattle, however, have a second structure that is involved in their fertility, a shrine called the *wagle* (fig. 9), which should also be avoided by women.

This takes the form of an inverted Y-shaped gateway to the central cattle-park, or sometimes to the compound of an individual. It is made of hard *peegyoh* wood and coloured with red ochre. To it are attached the skulls of cattle slaughtered at festivals and on occasion offerings of blood or beer are made 'to the souls of the cattle' by being poured over them. When questioning whether the souls of cattle are in the skulls, in the cattle-stones, in both or in neither, it is almost impossible to obtain a clear

Figure 9

answer. As always, when faced with a culturally inappropriate question, Dowayos reply: 'How could we know? We have not seen', as if they were the most hard-line positivists.

The second division of animals, the 'beasts of the bush', are treated quite differently. Although all men may hunt, not all men are 'true hunters' (*taabyaayo*) — specialists in this art — just as 'true cultivators' specialise in agriculture. Once again, this is a prescriptive, not a descriptive, category. Hunters' compounds are marked by special shrines decorated with the horns, neck, or skulls of animals they have killed. When not in use, a hunter's bow must be hung from this shrine, the *namyaagyo*,[8] and lustrations of blood, beer and plants must be made to ensure good fortune. This bow is very dangerous to others, especially to women. A man carrying such a bow should not even greet a woman. Pregnant or menstruating women are to be avoided absolutely. If contact is totally inevitable, a man should lay the bow down on the ground behind him before speaking. The alternative is menorrhagia, miscarriage and the bow would be spoiled, incapable of the simplest shot. A hunter must refrain from intercourse before going out into the bush. Should his fortune be suspiciously bad, or his aim impaired, he will suspect his wife of adultery and she will risk a beating. It is explained that animals would smell the adultery on him, game animals would flee, but snakes, leopards and scorpions would home in on him and pursue him relentlessly. Hunting is totally incompatible with pastoralism. A hunter, like a blacksmith, has 'hot hands' from the blood of dead animals and cannot keep cattle himself or they would perish.

The *namyaagyo* shrine is where the hunter returns after a kill. Not all animals necessitate this, only deer and buffalo — 'cattle-like' animals — require such treatment. The shrine is outside the village, in the bush, and made of Y-shaped pieces of *sathutu* ('farting wood') painted with red and black rings. It may also be decorated with *yaahutu* (sorcerer's shit) bark and rotten eggs. After killing, the hunter is required to eat the cooked throat of the animal he has killed before the *namyaagyo*. This is called 'the part of the bow'. The head is then placed on the shrine. Usage varies between the high mountains (Kpan) and the environs of Poli (Kongle). In the former, the heads and neck-bones remain on the shrine. In the latter, the head is later removed and burnt, to destroy it utterly. The neck-bone then replaces it. Usages vary according to skull-houses and the treatment of variation raises a considerable problem in analysis. Sometimes, one version of a ritual may be only an abbreviated form of another and questioning will reveal that this is known. Alternatively, relations may be much more complex. This differential treatment of the skulls of wild beasts will be further analysed when we look at the *sumoh* (death drum) at a later stage (p. 44).

We now have enough information to begin mapping the relations between these domains. Human fertility is clearly opposed to that of animals. The shrines and stones that ensure animal reproduction gravely interfere with human sexuality. The death of animals likewise has grave repercussions on the grounds of its similarity to menstruation which, as we have seen, is failed conception, flowing blood. Similarly, we should note that any infringement of the rules of human sexuality, in the form of adultery, has implications for the punctuation of the world. Domestic animals would be barren as the cattle-stones would disappear into the bush. On the other hand, bush animals 'like cattle' would vanish and the hunter would himself become the quarry of wild beasts. The world would be upside down.

Such effects are based upon the assumption that relations between these domains must be especially carefully handled because they are so similar that they constantly interfere with each other. The animals for whom the *namyaagyo* is set up are 'like cattle'. One does not offer there when one has killed a porcupine. Similarly, the stones of the cattle are 'like' the skulls of the ancestors and are handled in a similar fashion. As Levi-Strauss might put it, metaphorical similarity is the source of contiguous danger.

Just as in the case of the relations between blacksmith, Dowayo and rainchief we found that the terms arranged themselves in an analogue gradient of:

rainchief : Dowayo : : Dowayo : blacksmith

so the dangers of contiguity between human, domesticated animal and wild beast mark out a series of analogies that we can formalise in fig. 10.

This has a decidedly incomplete look. If the assumptions of structuralism about the nature of cultural symbolism are to carry any weight, they should give a better return than this and we may reasonably expect further levels of structure that either fill in or otherwise motivate the blanks. Let us look at this further.

If the distinction between cattle and humans relies upon a pre-existing similarity, we may hope to learn something from those occasions where this is stressed. At times, there is a clear identification of a man and his cattle. For example the genitals of male cattle are particularly prone to infection by parasites and the remedy for this is castration. The bloated

Humans		skulls in skull-house
Cattle	skulls on *wagle*	stones in pot
Wild beasts	skulls on *namyaagyo*	

Figure 10

testicles are then buried in the grove where boys are circumcised and, if several cattle are afflicted, the whole operation may well be carried out there by the circumciser. Dowayos quite consciously relate this to circumcision but contrast the cattle, who have to be held and complain loudly, with the brave candidate, who stands fast, without complaint, while he is cut.[9]

Again, when a rich man dies, several of his cattle may be killed to provide skins to wrap his corpse and provide meat for his kin. The death of men and cattle go hand in hand. The identification is stressed by restrictions on the kinds of cattle that may be killed and their manner of consumption. If it is the chief man of a hamlet who dies, the lead steer of the herd is the first to be killed. The beast's head is smeared with red ochre, as is the head of the dead man, and the skin is placed over his body with the animal's head against the chief's head. Only male cattle can be killed and they must be without blemish or deformity. The meat will be eaten by the dead man's brothers of circumcision, men who were circumcised at the same time as him. Women and uncircumcised boys can have no part of it.

Since women are physically exchanged for cattle, it is hardly surprising that they are occasionally identified with these animals. If a man is leading brideprice cattle to his parents-in-law's village, if the cattle seem reluctant, it is a sign that his wife will not stay with him long. If a cow given in brideprice is inadvertently tied up, this will prevent the wife bearing children.

As a final example, let us note the climax of the skull-ceremony where a man dances carrying the skulls of his dead ancestors on his head. Beside him dance men wearing the skins of the killed cattle, with the heads of the animals covering their own faces and kept in place by gripping the raw flesh between their teeth. At the end of the festival the skulls of the cattle are placed alongside those of the dead men on the *wagle*.

We may now fill in one of the blanks in fig. 10 to give fig. 11. It is interesting to see that identification centres on the sexual parts and the heads. I shall devote the next chapter to a more detailed consideration of this matter.

Humans	skulls on *wagle* (during skull festival)	skulls in skull-house
Cattle	skulls on *wagle*	stones in pot
Wild beasts	skulls on *namyaagyo*	

Figure 11

3 Some problems of the representational model of symbolism

In chapter 2, I looked at some aspects of symbolism as a punctuation of culture into domains, as a system of similar patterns. I should like to move on to a consideration of representational symbolism, which is what the man in the street tends to mean by symbolic analysis. Most of anthropology's standard approaches to symbolism are based upon linguistic models. The representational model relies – often unconsciously – on a naive notion of word meaning. A typical exponent of the genre is Victor Turner. For Turner (1967: 19) ritual is composed of symbols. Symbols are things 'regarded by general consent as naturally typifying or representing or recalling something by possession of analogous qualities or by association in fact or thought'.

In other words, symbols are meaningful and motivated. The word 'motivation' recalls Saussure, the source of most semiological theory. In treating language, Saussure (1974: 69) begins by excluding onomatopoeia, the linkage of sound and sense. He is operating entirely within language as a system of arbitrary signs. But, while he insists strongly on the arbitrary nature of the linguistic sign (1974: 67), he has a great deal to say about motivation. He allows that words may be relatively motivated (1974: 131) i.e. that although Fr. *dix* and *sept* are arbitrary, their product *dix-sept* is not. His conclusion (1974: 133) is interesting:

In a certain sense – one which must not be pushed too far but which brings out a particular form that the opposition may take – we might say that languages in which there is least motivation are more *lexicological*, and those in which there is greatest are more *grammatical*. Not because 'lexical' and 'arbitrary' on the one hand and 'relative motivation' on the other, are always synonymous, but because they have a common principle. The two extremes are like two poles between which the whole system moves, two opposing currents which share the movement of language: the tendency to use the lexicological instrument (the unmotivated sign) and the preference given to the grammatical instrument (structural rules).

Comparing this with Turner (above) we note a great difference. The elements with which Turner is concerned are much closer to onomatopoeia, in that they appeal directly to sense qualities, than any other area for which we have a linguistic model. It will be recalled that this is precisely the area that Saussure has already dismissed from his study. It would seem that we can usefully distinguish two forms of motivation – internal and external.[10] The first makes an appeal purely to structural rules. It is the sort of motivation that is encapsulated in the rules of a generative grammar in its simplest form. Given an initial element, it can be fed through a series of rules that map it onto a surface structure.[11] Saussure (1974: 161) already deals with it under the name of 'analogy'. The second form of motivation makes appeal to the outside world, the world of sense qualities and encyclopaedic knowledge in an unstructured form (Hays 1970). Although Saussure has boldly kicked this down the front steps, he allows it in again by the back door in his notion of 'folk etymology' whereby the arbitrary becomes at least relatively motivated. We should not forget that motivation is a relative matter.[12]

But the fact that Saussure has already dismissed onomatopoeia is not without consequences for general semiological enquiry. As he notes of this phenomenon:

> Once these words have been introduced into the language, they are to a certain extent subjected to the same evolution – phonetic, morphological etc. – that other words undergo . . . obvious proof that they lose something of their original character in order to assume that of the linguistic sign in general, which is unmotivated.   (1974: 69)

In other words, because Saussure is operating exclusively within the system of *langue*, his material is already internally motivated, regardless of external levels of motivation. This should alert us to the fact that it is unlikely that we are going to find the two forms of motivation in isolation in matters of symbolic analysis. Thus, to feel obliged to choose between the standard 'word-oriented' style of British anthropology (externally motivated) or the 'structural' style of French anthropology (internally motivated) is like deciding that all art must be either totally representational or wholly non-figurative. Obviously, one does not rule out the other and differences in emphasis may be more than a matter of the bias of the observer and correspond to some real differences in cultural style.

Where, then, do the schemata of chapter 2 fit into such an analysis? We cannot doubt that there is a heavy emphasis on internal motivation, lending itself to representation in the form of geometrically regular diagrams. All these are more or less explicitly derived from static phonological forms of what used to be known as 'structural linguistics' originating more in the phonology of Trubetzkoy than that of Saussure,[13] but corresponding quite clearly to Saussure's notions of analogy. The basic point is that the relationship between rainchief and Dowayo corresponds to that between Dowayo and blacksmith in exactly the same way that, in the phonological series of English consonants, /p/ is to /b/ as /t/ is to /d/, regardless of external constraints.

The degree of internal motivation of figs. 10 and 11, i.e. their underlying regularity, has still not been established and it is to this that I now return via a digression on Dowayo pots. I shall begin by examining how far relations of simple external motivation are sufficient to account for the nature of the uses to which pots are put in Dowayo culture. This will oblige us to consider the internal motivation that will be depicted in the form of diagrams developed from figs. 10 and 11. As is the nature of symbolic analysis, I shall be obliged to range rather widely over the ethnographic data before synthesising them.

Pots, it will be recalled, are made exclusively by the blacksmith women, who are also the principal midwives. There appear to be a number of clear examples of external motivation of the crassest 'A represents B' sort. A jar has a 'belly' (*buuyo*), 'neck' (*durkoh*) and 'mouth' (*yāayo*). Each pot has a decoration on the belly. This comes in three forms (fig. 12) but always in a star-shaped overall pattern. The chevron form is recognised as the only traditional form. An alternative decoration (fig. 13) arranges alternate bands of ornamentation and undecorated surface.

The same chevron decoration is used on the human face and belly. In the case of both pots and humans these markings are referred to as *gbeehtyo* 'scars'. They were traditionally cut into human flesh by the blacksmith (whose wife cuts them into the surface of the pots).

There are a number of cases of clear identification of the human belly with the belly of pots. It will be recalled that if a rainchief walks through a village when a potter is firing her pots, they will all break. Similarly, pots

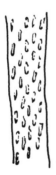  

Figure 12

cannot be made during the rainy season lest they break, i.e. the rainchief has a temporal as well as a spatial location. There is an absolute interdiction, however, during firing, on the potter drinking water, i.e. putting it in her belly. All these reduce to the incompatibility of the blacksmith's belly and what we may term 'moving water'.

It is in this context that we must also consider the disease that I mentioned earlier (p. 13) that is communicated by blacksmiths. This is a member of the class of diseases known as *zaase* 'dirt', 'pollution'.

This particular *zaase* comes in two forms, the male and the female. In the case of men, it causes a prolapsed anus (piles?). In women, it leads to what can only be called an ingrowing vagina. Its cause is the implements of smithing and potting. Especially dangerous is the blacksmith's bellows, a large phallic installation that must not be seen when glowing red hot (fig. 14). Of almost equal danger is the process of making pots. It is typical of *zaase* maladies that the cause and the cure are closely associated. Thus, in the present case, the cure for the female version of the disease is to rub the afflicted part with the glaze and smooth it with the tools used to finish off pots.

For any post-Freudian Westerner, it is impossible not to see the circumcised penis in the blacksmith's bellows. Given the equation of female belly and pot, and the putative similarity of bellows and penis, we might rather expect the male *zaase* to be reflected in the form of an affliction of the penis, gonorrhoea for example. This would give us fig. 15, in accordance with external resemblances (external motivation). How then are we to explain that male *zaase* afflicts the anus? There seems no *prima facie* evidence of similarity between bellows and anus. Ths first thing to note is that we are in the presence of a basic binary opposition between the two terms 'ingrowing vagina' and 'outgrowing anus', i.e. internal motivation is also structuring the system in play. Secondly, we must relate notions of *zaase* to two different versions of circumcision.

The Dowayos practise an extreme form of circumcision where the penis

Figure 13

is peeled for almost its entire length. This may happen at any age from about ten to twenty-five, and there is nothing to prevent an uncircumcised man marrying or a man being circumcised with his son. The precise origin of circumcision and its place in the Dowayo world will have to be looked at in a later chapter (p. 60), but it must be mentioned here that males and females have different 'official' versions of what happens. Women are told that the circumcision festival does not involve the penis at all (they are forbidden to see a circumcised penis on pain of death). It involves, rather, the anus which is sealed with a piece of cowhide. Thereafter a man never needs to defecate or break wind. In the dry season, when the vegetation has shrivelled up, Dowayoland is full of men strolling aimlessly around, plucking absently at trees, until the coast is clear so that they can dive behind a rock to relieve themselves. In fact, one of the most appreciated forms of all-male humour is a well-executed fart as an allusion to the reality of circumcision. In truth, the women know full well what happens at circumcision and are not fooled by the weak explanations offered by

Figure 14

Pot : belly : : bellows : penis

Figure 15

their menfolk when they are afflicted by diarrhoea at the change of season ('the skin must have rotted'). None of them, however, would risk admitting it publicly and the pretence is kept up rather like the supposed existence of Father Christmas before infants. Like most aspects of Dowayo life it becomes the subject of light banter between the sexes.[14]

The affliction of the male anus must then be viewed as a secondary displacement of the penis through a meeting of the two views of circumcision. Let it be noted how far this is from being a case of simple, external motivation. We must at least allow for 'interferences'.

A more complex case occurs at the skull-festival. At one stage, two special water-jars are taken from the skull-house and from the batch of women's skulls out in the bush. These are called *looreyo* 'soul', 'spirit', and are similar to ordinary water-jars in every respect except that they are decorated with small horns (fig. 16). One jar is regarded as female and stood on a hearth, the other as male and stood on the ground.[15] Fermenting beer is poured into each and the names of the dead for whom the skull-ceremony is being celebrated are called out. A little beer brought by all classes of relatives must be included. 'See, we have brought you beer. Come and accept it,' they cry. The bubbling of the beer is thought to be

Figure 16

the spirits of the dead. 'Why are you angry and pouring out only to one side?' After the festival, they will be covered with oil and ochre, like the important human participants, and be taken back to the skulls. But there is one basic difference between male and female jars. While the female jar must be intact, the male jar is pierced and has a wooden plug.[16] When the jar has been filled with beer, this is removed to allow the beer to flow all over the earth. The wholeness of the female jar poses no problems. It is clearly in the interests of the women to have wombs that are good vessels and retain their contents. As for the male pot, women never see it and it could be that the plugged jar, which is opened up only before males, recalls the male secret of circumcision, the plug in their anuses that is not there.

There is another possibility here. It should be noted that the pouring into the male jar is executed by the dead man's *duuse* (approx. 'great-grandfather', see below p. 71), a class of joking relative, aided by trans-vestite clowns. The pouring is carried out under a *sēko* (*Boswellia dalziellii*), which is what the widows are wearing at this festival. The pouring into the female jar occurs under a *tarko* tree which otherwise has strong male con-notations, being one of the trees under which circumcision can occur. The precise nature of Dowayo plant symbolism is still ill-mapped and it would be unwise to rely too heavily upon it; but, given the general ambience of joking and reversal that obtains at the skull-festival, we might well be in the presence of anti-motivation. When studying internal motivation (e.g. the simple binary opposition as between male and female *zaase* above) it has been quite important while it has not played any role in the study of external motivation. This is surprising given its great antiquity and wide occurrence outside anthropology. Consider, for example, the common etymological technique of explanation by opposites used by both Greeks and Romans. The Greek *lithos* 'stone' is derived by ancient workers on language from the phrase *lian theein* 'to run too much' because this is what a stone does *not* do. Equally *lucus* 'grove' is derived from *lucende* 'being light' on the grounds that this is what a grove is *not*. We know this form of motivation as irony but it recurs at all levels of cultural classification e.g. the nickname 'Little John' for a big man, the shaggy dog story which is funny because it isn't a joke, etc. There is no reason *a priori* why this form of motivation might not be invoked in ritual matters. But let us return to the matter of jars and bellies.

There is another festival, *rohtumyo* 'decoration', celebrated after the death of a woman.[17] While her skull-ceremony is organised by her lineal relatives, her jar-festival is in the hands of her husband or children. The dead woman's water-jar spends the night in her compound. It is filled with millet-beer and all women linked by kinship or friendship come and offer a pinch of germinated millet flour causing rapid bubbling in the jar. Again, this is taken as evidence of the presence of the spirit of the dead woman.

Her patrilineal relatives call out her name given at birth. Others call out the other names she may have assumed during her life.[18] Old women lick the jar 'to get fat', young women 'to get pregnant'. The jar is then half-emptied and dressed up (fig. 17) in a fashion recalling that of a circumcision candidate, in burial cloth, skins etc. (fig. 18). The jar is carried from the compound and a man puts it on his head to dance with it. Afterwards, in west Dowayoland, it is smeared with oil and ochre, undressed at the crossroads and carried back to the brothers' village where it is preserved in a hut with an unbeaten floor. In east Dowayoland, however, the jar is placed in the bush with the skulls of the women ancestors. Although a hat is attached to the jar, a 'head' is previously fashioned for it out of a millet stick and padding.

The detail of the unbeaten floor, insisted upon by informants, in the west, is interesting. Questioning rapidly enters the vicious circle the fieldworker comes to know well. 'Why must the floor be unbeaten?' 'Because it would be bad.' 'Why would it be bad?' 'Because the ancestors told us so.' 'Why did the ancestors tell you so?' 'Because it would be bad.'

The preparation used to harden floors comes from the tree *Tarekopse* 'Fulani thorns' which has strong associations with circumcision (see below

Figure 17

p. 60). This is also the tree used to seal a leaking jar by wiping a decoction of its leaves over the belly of the vessel. We may note at this point that huts have 'heads', 'mouths' and 'bellies' too. The use of the names of the bodily parts for the metonymic dissection of other objects is a widespread linguistic habit among the Dowayos.[19]

If we compare the male and female bodily cavities according to the official ideology we find (fig. 19) a classification that plays on the distinction ópen/closed. Female III would seem merely to be a weakened repetition of female II.

I stated earlier that the jar festival was performed for a married woman (and all Dowayo women marry) by her husband or children. But an abbreviated form of it is performed for an unmarried girl by her parents, as it is for an uncircumcised boy. Dowayo uncircumcised are classed with women. They are buried with them, barred from specifically masculine areas such as the skull-house and circumcision grove and mocked for 'smelling like women'. Circumcision functions to remove this female aspect of the adult male. It is in keeping with the official ideology that this should be marked by the change in vessels from one marked for 'openness' to one marked for 'closure'. But the attribution to a boy of what we

Figure 18

have been indicating as a womb, albeit in only the most abstract sense, creates something of a problem and raises the suspicion that the view 'pots are bellies' may be inadequate. The mapping of the 'open/closed' oppo- sition onto the container of the container i.e. the hut in which they are kept, might seem explicable in a number of ways:

(1) redundancy: the reduplication of features that is often attributed to symbolic systems (Needham 1962: 309—10);
(2) an example of secondary displacement as in the case of the black- smith's *zaase* in males (above);
(3) further representational symbolism whereby the hut becomes itself representative of the human body.

Possibilities 1 and 2 are not really distinct. In as far as pots, unless flawed, are unsealed, this aspect of their structure could never become a stressed feature. Huts, however, are normally sealed and the omission of this treat- ment constitutes a deliberate act. Redundancy is indeed a characteristic of Dowayo ritual. For example, the placing of the women's *looreyo* jar on a hearth simply stresses a feature already implicit in the opposition to the male jar.

In fact, 3 cannot be opposed to 1 and 2 either. All statements in terms of 3 can be rephrased in terms of the other two possibilities as far as this particular case is concerned. One could only choose between them by establishing whether or not the equation of house and human body is a standard theme of Dowayo symbolism and therefore to be recommended on the grounds of the generality, comprehensiveness and simplicity of the resulting description. In fact, as can be seen especially from a consider- ation of insulting behaviour between brothers of circumcision and the ritual of Appendix I (m), this approach has much to recommend it.

Human body:

male I	female II
totally sealed	open but unflawed vessel

The comparison of the *looreyo* vessels gives us:

male II	female II
sealed but openable kept in sealed skull-house	open but unflawed kept in open air

The jar-festival container gives us:

	female III
	open and unflawed kept in unsealed hut

Figure 19

We seem to be here in the presence of a 'theme', like onomatopoeia, again an image derived from poetics rather than linguistics proper.

As regards crediting a boy with a symbolic 'womb', this can be viewed as the transference of ritual from an area where external motivation is strong, through other internal equations of the symbolic system (i.e. uncircumcised : circumcised : : female : male), to an area where external motivation no longer holds. We shall see other examples of this when looking at the festivals.

If several examples of behaviour occur, tending – at least at first sight – to lend credence to the equation of pots and bellies, there are also clear examples of the equation of pots and heads.

It will be recalled that two forms of overall design occur on water-jars, the star form (fig. 20) and the alternating band form (fig. 13). The first is reproduced on the heads of widows at the *taabfāakyo* 'sticking of the bow' ceremony where their husband's bow is fixed under the roof of the men's skull-house (fig. 21). The hair is trimmed with a razor-blade into a distinctive star shape.

At the jar-ceremony of a dead woman, it is her husband, daughters and 'sisters of the village' (women of about her age, particularly those who

Figure 20

began menstruating at the same time as she did) who adopt the star tonsure. Boys adopt either this tonsure or one that reproduces the striped decoration of fig. 13 for the ceremony of the 'entry to the skull-house' when the recently circumcised are permitted to enter the skull-house for the first time (fig. 22).

It is in the case of the rainchief of Mango, however, that the identification is firmest. Whereas all other Dowayos remove the skulls of the dead and ultimately place them, in the case of circumcised males, in the bush in skull-houses, the rainchiefs adopt a different practice. The skull-house of the Mango rainchief contains water-jars (fig. 23). These are of various sorts. There is a single lumpy red jar called *dolnoyoh* 'old female jar', surrounded by lesser similar jars, *dolwaato* 'son jars'. Apart, is a large smooth jar, 'the old man' *dentio*. The first give the heavy female and the light male rain respectively. The last gives *gbāa tiryo* 'hail'. Inside each are special stones. When a Mango rainchief dies, his head may not be removed for fear of causing a flood, nor must relatives cry or torrential rain would result. The body is left intact and a special water-jar is made to replace the head and kept in a shelter inside the main compound. Men and women are mixed together. The skull-festival and jar-ceremonies are not celebrated

Figure 21

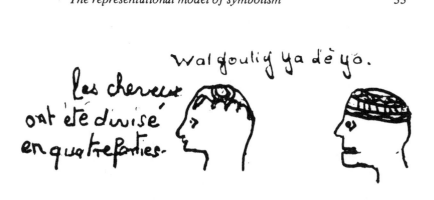

Figure 22 Sketch by a Dowayo youth

Figure 23

here. If there is any need to offer to the spirit of a particular relative, instead of throwing the offering on his skull, it is placed on his water-jar.

At the village of the other main rainchief, at Kpan, the procedure is somewhat different. Heads are removed, but are buried again on the mountain called *Waaduufi* 'The soft spot on the top of a boy's head'. At the summit of this is a white stone. By removing this, the Old Man of Kpan could cause a flood that would inundate the whole world. The Old Man of Kpan said that, in the time of his grandfather, heads were not removed at all in the village. The practice had been introduced by his father. There are no skull-ceremonies at Kpan, nor do jar-ceremonies occur. Should an offering to a particular spirit be necessary, it is made on the first stone that covers a Dowayo grave. At Kpan, too, there are three sorts of rain-stones, 'male', 'female' and 'boy', each associated with slightly different classes of rain and buried by the heads of dead rainchiefs.

Let us now turn back to fig. 11 (p. 20). Cattle are 'repaired' by the skulls on the *wagle* and the stones in a pot. Wild beasts seem anomalous in that their fertility is maintained only by the hard body parts on the *namyaagyo*. It is at this point that we should note that the rainchiefs claim to possess stones to 'repair' them. (These are not only for 'cattle-like' beasts of the bush but also for such creatures as the mountain porcupine that greatly ravages the fields of Dowayos. The Old Man of Kpan is particularly credited with authority over these animals. After he had a disagreement with his wife's brother over his legendary unwillingness to provide brideprice payments, this unfortunate man's fields were almost totally destroyed by a group of these rapacious beasts who tore up all his groundnuts and chewed his melons. It was universally assumed that this was due to the Old Man's manipulation of the porcupine-stones, and he himself did nothing to refute such a view.)

We are justified, then, in entering a new term in fig. 11 to give fig. 24.

In the 'human' category, adjustments must also be made. In the 1942 annual report the chef de subdivision of Poli regrets the lack of success in recruiting soldiers among the Dowayos on the grounds that they refuse foreign service through fear that their skulls will not be returned to their proper skull-houses. Whether this was anything more than a convenient excuse may be doubted. Certainly, modern Dowayos are unconcerned

Humans	skulls on *wagle* (during skull-festival)	skulls in skull-house
Cattle	skulls on *wagle*	stones in pot
Wild beasts	skulls on *namyaagyo*	stones in pot

Figure 24

about the return of skulls. The missing head is simply replaced by a stone. The same happens should it be impossible to retrieve the skull of a man killed in a fall, or if the head should disintegrate before the celebration of its skull-festival. In the case of the Mango rainchief, the head is replaced by a pot. In the case of Kpan, it is replaced by a stone on the mountain whose name is part of the skull i.e. a stone whose metaphorical 'skull' quality is heavily marked. We can produce this as fig. 25.

The broad internal motivation of the system cannot, I think, be denied. There is a basic bifurcation between skulls and stones in all domains except the human. If we wish to look at this in terms of 'meaning', it seems quite clear that this lends itself to a description in strongly mechanistic terms, invoking Dowayo notions of spirit. The skulls would 'represent' the relatively hard, permanent parts of living beings of known individuality. The stones would 'represent' the permanent 'pool' of spirit from which came and to which returned all life. The slow decay of the skulls 'represents' their conversion back to the stones. Many aspects of Dowayo life and ritual would be justified by such a theory, e.g. the notion that killing game in some undefined way increases general fertility, the yet to be considered problem of human slaying to celebrate the skull-festival. In the case of cattle, it can be claimed that Dowayos *do* have something approximating to such a causal theory and can explain it even to a visiting anthropologist. In the case of wild beasts, they have nothing like an articulate causal view. The case of humans is, understandably, more complex.

The distinction between stone and skull is replaced by a purely temporal one between skull up to the moment of placement on the *wagle* and skull afterward. This maintains the difference between the two categories, however, in that it clearly constitutes the line between differentiated and undifferentiated humanity. The career of a Dowayo skull is represented in fig. 26. It resolves itself into a series of plays on the oppositions: up/down, inside/outside.

More interestingly, it is only up to the placement on the *wagle* that each individual among the male dead is referred to by his name(s). These are called out when the beer is poured for men and women at the skull-festival and for women alone at the jar-festival.[20] Relations of implication

Human

skulls on *wagle*	skulls in skull-house
stones (skulls lost)	stones (skulls lost)
pot in village (Mango)	stone in pot (Mango)
	stone/skull (Kpan)

Figure 25

and exclusion between jar- and skull-ceremonies vary from one skull-house to another. Amongst some, the jar-ceremony may not be performed once the skull-ceremony is over. The individuality of the woman is then over. In other areas of Dowayoland, it is the jar-ceremony that marks the end of her differentiated existence, since women's remains are not actually placed on the *wagle*. Their skulls are simply dumped to one side. At the end of the ceremony, the skulls of both men and women are given their final resting places, heaped indiscriminately in big beer-jars or tipped into pits in the ground. Henceforth, if the spirit of one of these deceased people troubles the living, offerings will be made to the whole jar as a unit or be simply flung on the outside of the skull-house or the top of the pit. In some skull-houses, after this point, the offerings are made to the *looreyo* water-jars that are kept with the skulls. The exact point where the line is drawn varies from one house to another, but — as far as I am aware — it is always drawn. The skulls pass from differentiated to undifferentiated.

What, then, of the complexities of the rainchiefs' skulls? These meet the demands of the simplest sort of internal motivation in that we are here concerned with constant rearrangements of the same elements, whether or not these arrangements themselves can be motivated in any way. The system shows the same tendency towards ending up at the 'stone' end, but there is interference from other levels of classification. In view of all that has been said, it now seems simplistic to talk, in this case, of simple identification between either pots and bellies or pots and heads. We have seen to what degree purely internal motivation may be involved. It is not easy, moreover, to distinguish in every case whether identification with head or belly fits the facts better, as far as the external levels are concerned.

For example, in the case of the woman's water-jar ritual, the spirit is

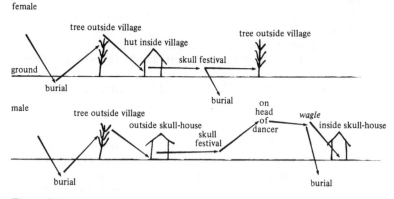

Figure 26

regarded as present in the pot, manifesting itself in the form of fermentation. Dowayo views of the world locate the spirit inherent in every human as housed in the head. For a spirit to be located in its own belly would be a monstrosity. The pot then might be regarded as a surrogate, culturally formed belly as would the *looreyo* jars; but their very location with the skulls suggests that we might view them more as a generalised image of a body cavity, be it head or belly, in either of which a spirit can lodge.

The same view of the body is implicit in Dowayo notions of 'headwitchcraft'. Although Dowayos have categories of witchcraft that involve plants or cause attacks by wild animals, the main form of witchcraft is 'headwitchcraft' (*zuulyaayo*). Witchcraft is communicated by kin in food, especially meat and peanuts, which are eaten by the individual who is to be infected with it. Thereafter, he or she becomes a witch. Witchcraft thus enters via the belly but dwells in the head and comes out at night to suck the blood of cattle or humans. It may be carried great distances under the wings of an owl and is said to resemble a chick. The sighting of an owl near a village is thus a matter for great alarm. Witchcraft, however, is hardly ever invoked as an explanation of disease; by far the greatest number of diseases are ascribed to the activities of ancestral spirits. When Dowayos declare that so-and-so was killed 'by witchcraft', they normally mean that he was a witch.

Witchcraft is pictured as greedy. It takes foolish risks in its thirst for blood, injuring itself on sharp anti-witchcraft medicines that a man may put around his cattle-park, threshing-floor or on the roof of his hut. It is especially dangerous for a witch to communicate his witchcraft to a male child before circumcision since he may die from contact with the knife, or to someone who goes to the city where his witchcraft may be excited by the displays of meat on butchers' slabs and injure itself on the sharp knives lying around.[21] All witchcraft remedies are either strong-smelling or spiky.[22] The spikiness of the rainpots is explained as repelling witchcraft or ancestral interference. The mountain porcupine, whose excrement is flung on the skulls at Daksidongo, is the foremost prophylactic against both evils, and its quills decorate both heads and roofs of huts.[23] In fact, it cannot be maintained that 'headwitchcraft' and ancestral invasion are kept strictly separate,[24] and both rely on the view of the body as a series of vessels that may be occupied by contents from without. The belly/jar/ hut/stone group constitutes a ritual category for which the language would have no term. We may at this point feel that a change of image is appropriate, shifting from a purely linguistic model to one from poetics. The ritual group could then be viewed as like a riddle image in folkloristic analysis. A metaphoric riddle (Barley 1974) works by presenting a hidden term in the form of a given term. Thus, for example, a Dowayo riddle:

I have a slave who does everything for me, in dry season and wet season. But when I come home, I throw him outside. The rain beats down on him, the sun burns him. But he says nothing. What is it?

Answer: Hoe

The riddle works by describing an inanimate tool as if it were the animate agent wielding it, i.e. it restructures our normal set of classifications and creates a mediating category that is neither hoe nor slave but simultaneously both or neither. Similarly, the processes of cultural symbolism we have been observing operate on the set jar/hut/skull/stone in a fashion that blurs them into a class that – if obliged to give it a name – we might term 'vessels of spirit'. But to approach symbols in the fashion of one solving a riddle is to ignore other forms of motivation since one never 'solves' any matter of cultural symbolism. One simply finds various ways in which the arbitrary may be converted to the motivated. Later on, I shall examine in depth one such 'cultural riddle' that is central to the ritual system. For the moment, let us simply note that the power of such images often lies precisely in their ability to maintain several simultaneous references without being clearly reducible to any one. Later, we shall also have to deal with elaborations of fig. 25 that further weaken the relative importance of external motivation.

Before turning to these, let us explore a further avenue opened up by representational symbolism suggested by the riddle image of this chapter.

4 The leopard cannot change his spots

If it were possible to use the simple representational model of the analysis of cultural symbols in anything but a trivial way — and I in no way rule out this possibility for other cultures which may be much more 'lexical' (Saussure 1974: 133) than the Dowayo — then this might happen in at least two ways. First, it might be possible to establish culture-wide themes. We can easily imagine a culture where pots clearly always 'were' wombs in any usage that we wished to term symbolic. The dreamed-of dictionary of symbols could be written instead of simply being assumed to exist, perhaps with one or two very large terms and a certain amount of polysemy and homonymity, but conforming to the exigencies of lexicographical semiology. To interpret a ritual, we should merely have to look up the entries of the symbols used, make some allowance for selectional limitations of meaning, interpret actions performed on/with them in terms of syntax and insert the whole into an appropriate context. This has at least the benefit of perhaps being susceptible to formalisation and being a sufficiently layered operation to give some scope for subtlety. A concentration on 'appropriate context' would give the Douglas (of 1975: 249) sort of interpretation; a concentration on the dictionary, the Turner (of 1967: 19).

A second approach, and one that must surely follow hotly upon the first, would be to examine the forms of equivalences postulated within the dictionary to determine whether there were any cultural patterning at this level. This operation could also be carried out by merely postulating local equivalences without invoking generalised themes.

One of the areas where this might most profitably be attempted in Dowayo culture is the minor folkloristic genres. In Britain, folklore studies are regarded by anthropologists with scornful condescension, and perhaps rightly so given the status of the subject as a relic of genteel rural enquiry. In the United States, things are very different and the subject seems to have a present and a future as well as a past. Folklorists work alongside anthropologists in research into such matters as verbal art and ritual, to their great mutual enrichment. Within this context, it is not the anachronism that it might at first appear, to consider such forms as proverbs in a work that purports to deal with cultural symbolism of an African people. We may recall Jakobson's (1966: 287) definition of the proverb as the 'minimal form of culture'. If we cannot deal with even this, then we cannot deal with anything.

Proverbs, like spells, are basically structuring genres, 'portable templates' (McLeod 1972) that impose the same structure on diverse contents through a pre-existing grid of very basic logical relationships. Let me explain this further by using an example I have employed elsewhere (Barley 1974).

Let us suppose we are discussing the fact that Albert Smith, previously convicted of theft, has committed the same offence again. We might comment: 'The leopard cannot change his spots'. Here we have a given term 'leopard' in terms of which we discuss a hidden term 'Albert Smith'. We are clearly in the presence of an analogy which we can break down as:

The leopard : his spots : : Albert Smith : his criminality

This deals with the external relations of these forms, the relations between given and hidden term. It also, however, points to the equally significant internal relations, the logical connection between 'spots' and 'leopard' that is mapped onto 'criminality' and 'Albert Smith'. It is precisely this relationship that makes up the context-free core of the proverb.

In the case in question, the relationship is that between a category and the distinctive features that define it. We may express the relationship, at its deepest level, as a maxim-type proposition:

One-time membership of category A implies permanent possession of distinctive feature *a*.

This may then be termed the structural description of this proverb. This does not, however, suffice to describe exhaustively the proverb in question. Much information made use of by the naive native proverb-user is still not represented here. We cannot, for example, know from the structural description alone that the hidden term of 'leopard' must be specified as 'animate'. 'Spots', on the other hand, cannot be used of a term of positive cultural value (e.g. 'truth', 'honesty' etc.) nor a concrete term. It can, however, refer to both singular and plural hidden terms. We should, therefore, have to include in a full description certain relevance restrictions defining categories between which such verbal forms can operate.[25]

This is a quite different concern from that of Arewa and Dundes (1964: 71):

In order to study the enthography [*sic*] of the speaking of folklore (or, ethnography of speaking folklore, more concisely), clearly one cannot be limited to texts. One needs texts in their contexts. One needs to ask not only for proverbs and what counts as a proverb, but also for information as to the other components of the situations in which proverbs are used. What are the rules governing who can use proverbs, or particular proverbs, and to whom? Upon what occasions? In what places? With what other persons present or absent? Using what channel (e.g. speaking, drumming etc.)? Do restrictions or prescriptions as to the use of proverbs or a proverb have to do with particular topics? With the specific relationship between speaker and addressee? What exactly are the contributing contextual factors which make the use of a proverb, or of a particular proverb, possible or not possible, appropriate or inappropriate?

They are much more concerned with factors of performance and not in the ways in which metaphor in a particular culture may be rule-governed.

As far as such minor forms are concerned in English, certain metaphoric equations are permitted and certain equations are not. Thus, one can talk about humans in terms of animals but not the reverse. Likewise, inanimate given terms presuppose animate (human or non-human) hidden terms. There seems to be a logical hierarchy (fig. 27).

In cultures that employ metaphorical verbal invocations, we might well find that the same selectional restrictions would hold (Barley 1974: 245). In Dowayoland such forms do not, however, occur; inanimate objects may be literally addressed as if possessed of reason but always in an unmetaphoric mode. Thus, to determine whether or not a man is guilty of some minor theft, he may be made to boil water in an ordinary pot.[26] The pot is addressed: 'If this man is guilty do not boil. If he is innocent, do so swiftly.' If the pot does not rapidly boil in a good rolling manner, he will be accounted guilty. It is unclear whether we should regard this as words having causal efficacy (Skorupski 1976: 102) or merely operative force defining the framework.

In Dowayoland, something that we can reasonably equate with our own class, 'proverbs', does exist.[27] Like many African peoples, the Dowayos greatly admire the appropriate use of such proverbs in debate and credit them with great persuasive effect. A good talker will have a ready stock of stereotyped forms. While it is often easy to see the structural description of

Given term

	inanimate	animate	human

Hidden term

	inanimate	animate	human
	animate	human	
	human		

Figure 27

a Dowayo proverb, the selectional restrictions had to be elicited by discussion with men in groups since they are not in accordance with the way an Englishman, calling on rules of relevance from his own culture, would apply them.

A man does not shit without his anus feeling it.

Maxim paraphrase: A person does not do something bad without knowing he has done it.

But this form is not used exclusively of people, as would be the case with an English proverb. I heard it used of dogs, for example. Similarly, we have the proverb:

Our hand does not refuse our anus.

Maxim paraphrase: Those who are close to us will not refuse us an unpleasant service. This, I heard used of matters as diverse as the incestuous behaviour of goats and the fine cutting qualities of a man's favourite knife.

While in Dowayoland, I collected about sixty such sayings and examined their relevance restrictions. From such a small sample, it may be illegitimate to draw firm conclusions, but it seems that the case may be that we should depict these relevance restrictions as in fig. 28.

To put it another way, whereas English divides up the world into these three categories that are kept distinct, or at least endowed with different metaphorical privileges, Dowayo allows free movement in all directions. Men may be thought of in terms of inanimate objects and vice versa. The principles that structure one domain will be expected to structure another, since this is what proverbs are all about. We should note that Dowayos are often described as 'animists'. They point out certain places, especially river-crossings and mountains, as dangerous and declare that offerings of beer or meat must be made there in return for safe passage. Only occasionally, however, do they invoke hostile spirits as the explanation, as they point out the broken vessels of those who had beer to offer but tried to sneak past without giving. As we have seen above in the case of the cattle-

Given term

	inanimate	animate	human
Hidden term			
	inanimate	inanimate	inanimate
	animate	animate	animate
	human	human	human

Figure 28

stones, it may be tempting to invoke unconsciously posited spirits as causal mechanisms but this may prove unnecessary if we can show internal motivation mapped from another domain. Thus, the 'animism' of the Dowayos falls into place as part of a wider tendency to use the same structure again and again regardless of content, ignoring the distinctions inanimate/animate/human, i.e. a question of cultural relevance restrictions.

A second approach that could be used in any completely open and formal approach to representational symbolism would be to examine the logical nature and distribution of the underlying processes. Dubois *et al.* (1970) have gone some way towards showing how this might be done. They posit two forms of decomposition of the world, π and Σ. These are, respectively, decomposition into parts, i.e. 'tree' can be divided up into trunk, leaves, root, branches, etc., and decomposition into semes, i.e. 'tree' can also be divided into different species, oak, beech, birch, etc. Combinations of these 'synecdoches' give different forms of metaphor. Thus, the local equation of a womb and a jar involves two-way Σ-synecdoche. A common feature 'container' of greater generality than either can be found, imputed to both and used to structure the relationship between them.[28] Semantic markers are erased (Katz and Fodor 1963; Dubois *et al.* 1970: 104) by particularising synecdoche to give the bridging category 'container' and reassigned by particularising synecdoche to identify the two categories 'womb' and 'jar'. (See also Barley 1974: 149.) This can be depicted as fig. 29.

A rather more complex case would be raised by the Dowayo identification between man and leopard on the grounds of shared features such as 'bloodshed', 'fierceness' etc. This example requires closer study.

When a man kills a leopard, the body is returned to the village and skinned. The skin is a valuable possession and needed for the rites of circumcision. The head is placed not on the *wagle* (see fig. 24), not on the *namyaagyo*, but on the *dōre* (fig. 30). This is a Y-shaped piece of *kābrio* wood set up in the middle of the public place. It is erected for three reasons only — for the skull-festival, for the slaying of an outsider and for the killing of a leopard. A leopard-killer (and a man-slayer both *nokbukyaayo*) must live in the public space for three days wearing

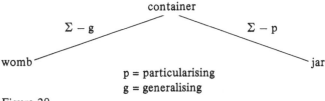

Figure 29

dalambo leaves, like a man in mourning,[29] then a white cloth, like a man coming out of mourning. He is fed the meat of wild animals or, in the case of a leopard-killer, the flesh of the leopard. He begins by eating the throat before the *dōre* and must be fed by another man- or leopard-killer. Such men (or their sons if they are dead) are fed the flesh of wild animals before the *dōre* during the skull-festival. After this, the *gapsnaabo* 'battle-song' is played before the *dōre*, as during the circumcision ceremony and after the slaying of a man. The man must then be given 'leopard's drops', a veg-etable remedy to put in his eyes to avoid blindness. The same holds for a man-killer. Henceforth the man may wear leopard's claws around his hat. Such a man is buried with *yaahutu*[30] 'sorcerer's shit' bark in his mouth and his sons bite on such bark during circumcision.

The head of the leopard is removed from the *dōre*. Some men told me that in former times (there have been no leopards in Dowayoland for thirty years) the skull underwent the full skull-ceremony and was placed in the skull-house with the other men's skulls.

Looking at fig. 24, we can locate the leopard halfway between wild beasts and humans, the categories it moves between. The skull of the leopard moves off towards human skulls, but it does not escape the 'gravi-tational pull' of the skull/neck/stone complex. Inside the *sumoh*, the drum

Figure 30

played for the deaths of men before the *dōre*, is a round stone called *naamkole* 'the leopard's neck'. This justifies us in viewing the leopard as in the latest revision of fig. 24, giving fig. 31.

This does not end the elaborations that the leopard undergoes. We must examine the linguistic evidence. The leopard is called *naamyo*, the lion *naamnoyoh* 'old female leopard'. Smaller *felidae* are called *naamwaatoh* 'sons of the leopard'. Dowayos also explain that these classes of animals are *pabis* (see fig. 3) 'MoBro-SiDa/SiSo'. A male lion would be *naamnoh-walo* 'male, old female leopard'.[31] When requested for 'baby, small *felidae*' Dowayos either give *naamwaatoh* or say there is no term. These smaller *felidae* are also called *roohbyo* and *dōgyo* (serval and civet cat (?) respectively). Leopard-skins are worn by circumcision candidates unless they are very small when they wear *roohbyo*-skins. *Dōgyo*-skins are worn by clowns. The scent gland makes a remedy to keep away spirits.

When working in this area, the linguistically inept anthropologist is wrestling with all sorts of clumsy notions, 'meaning', 'translation', 'literal', 'metaphorical', all of which threaten to undermine the whole proceeding by their crass ethnocentrism. Exasperated by my questioning, by queries as to whether a 'lion' ('old female leopard') and a 'leopard' mated to produce 'small *felidae*' ('sons of the leopard'), they always told the same story.[32]

Myth 1
A leopard (*naamyo*) took a lion (*naamnoyoh*) as wife. They lived in a cave in the mountains and had three children (*naamwaato*). One day the leopard roared. Two children were afraid and ran away. They became the *roohbyo* and *dōgyo*. The one who stayed became a leopard. It is finished.

When I asked whether this happened only once or whether these things still happened, I received answers representing all positions between these two extreme possibilities. For some, the *roohbyo* was the true child of the leopard, while the *dōgyo* was not, for others: 'We do not know, we have not seen it.' But the area is clearly structured. However this comes out in explanations, these animals are related:

> Leopard to lesser *felidae* : : men to children : : bold to fearful.

In everyday language a bold assertive man is called a 'leopard'.

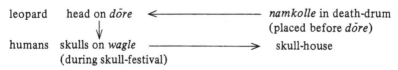

Figure 31

In the archives at Poli is an undated report concerning deaths of boys who have disappeared. The French colonial officer enquiring into their whereabouts was told: 'They were eaten by leopards.' It is clear that he suspects foul play and some hideous ritual. Such stories about the Dowayos are still common among white missionaries and ex-administrators. However, it is when a boy dies as a result of the extreme suffering of circumcision that his mother is told: 'He was eaten by leopards.'

Let us try to bring some of this together.

The leopard has been located (provisionally) between wild beasts and men. The man who kills it is treated as a human-killer. The treatment of the leopard is half way between that of a man and that of a wild beast, being influenced by both structures. Dowayo equations of leopard and human centre on shared attributes of fierceness and bloodshed. This is our double Σ-synecdoche as in fig. 32.

In fact, the position is more complicated than this. The features shared by leopard and man are much more numerous. Dowayos, for example, when describing the leopard, make much of the fact that it drags its prey up a tree to eat it. The result is that it leaves the skulls of its victims in the forks of trees, just as Dowayos leave their dead (see fig. 26). The leopard, moreover, undergoes total π-synecdochic dissection. Its claws adorn the skull of a killer. Its skin adorns the circumcision candidate. Its 'son' adorns the lowest 'sorcerer', the clown. Its 'neck' goes in the death drum. Circumcisers leap out on the youths they are going to cut, grunting 'like leopards'. At the death of a circumciser they use a bull-roarer to scare away women. This is said to sound like the roar of a leopard. The skull-house sorcerer has a special hook made of the root of the tree whose leaves are worn by a leopard-killer (*dalambo*).[33] This can cure blindness, the disease that is incurred by killing a leopard. Sorcerers have a special name for it — *naamorko* 'leopard's claw' — which is what it most closely resembles.

As well as being a dangerous and hostile animal, the leopard is also a mountain dweller. The rainchief, the Old Man of Kpan, is credited with the ability to turn into a leopard. After his death, when his head is buried, his spirit will emerge from the grave in the form of a wild cat or leopard. His relatives, the Masters of the Earth at Daksidongo, likewise become leopards after death. At the skull-festival at Daksidongo, the first

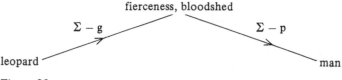

Figure 32

excrement thrown on the skulls must be that of the mountain porcupine.
This will attract the spirits to the mountains and away from men. Otherwise there is danger that they will appear as leopards and kill the cattle of
their descendants. A recent outbreak of fowl-pest that destroyed most of
the poultry in a large area of Dowayoland was attributed to the failure to
take this precaution at the last skull-festival celebrated there. It is the scent
gland of the leopard or 'sons of leopards' that is the principal ingredient of
the remedy against witchcraft.

If there is an equation between leopard and man, precisely who is concerned? We note that both the candidate of circumcision and the cutter
are involved. If we wish to phrase it in terms of thematic meaning, we can
say that it is man in his wild aspect that is involved here, man as killer,
shedder of blood, slayer of beasts, murderer; man as liminal, bush-dwelling
and dangerous. Synecdochic dissection and retotalisation give us a picture
as in fig. 33.

In effect, the relatively simple picture of fig. 32 is replaced by the
physical dismemberment of the leopard (π-g) and association with an
aspect of 'wild man' (Σ-p). There is clearly a strong element of opposition
with 'man as domesticated beast' that comes with the identification of a
man with his cattle. Once again, wherever we find strong external motivation in Dowayo culture, it is always within a field structured by internal
relations.

Looking at the features brought together by fig. 33, we note that there
comes a point at which the arbitrary enters. Features of 'the wild aspect of
man' tie up with various odds and ends of the physical leopard but in an
ill-defined way. The assignation of elements itself is relatively arbitrary.
There seems no reason why the smell rather than the noise of the leopard
should associate with witchcraft.[34] One motivates as best one can. There
is, of course, no *a priori* reason why motivation should cease at any particular stage of the operation and it is to be expected that different cultures will draw the line at different points. Motivation is far from an all-or-
nothing business. (See note 12.)

The different 'feel' of various cultures may have much to do with the
different points at which they decide their task of motivation to be over.

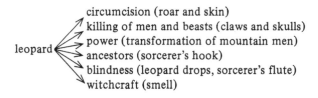

leopard
- circumcision (roar and skin)
- killing of men and beasts (claws and skulls)
- power (transformation of mountain men)
- ancestors (sorcerer's hook)
- blindness (leopard drops, sorcerer's flute)
- witchcraft (smell)

Figure 33

The example of the leopard raises another point. According to Dubois *et al.* (1970), the only synecdochic couplings permitted in language are either two-way π-, or two-way Σ- synecdoches. Mixing is not permissible as it generates nonsense. In practice, of course, such arrangements *are* found, but only in poetry where they are lumped together with other tropes under the catch-all title metonymy or association.

One of these non-permissible combinations much used by Dowayos is π-p plus Σ-g (plus Σ-p). In note 31 I dealt with the linguistic terms -*noyoh* 'old woman' and -*walo* 'male'.

As I mentioned at that time, this is a binary split that structures many domains of Dowayo language, female being always the larger, more general category. This seems to be a case of gender following sex. The opposition -*noyoh* / -*walo* is correlated with two others — round / extended and black / red. Such is the case with the rain-stones. The *dōre* itself is divided into male and female parts, the female being rounded, the male pointed. In some parts of Dowayoland the *dōre* is made of stone. In this case, the male part is tall, thin, red, the female squat, round, black. After circumcision, the male member is covered with red scar-tissue that only blackens as a man ages, and this motivates the same distinctions. The penis sheath worn over most of Dowayoland by circumcised males is a tubular gourd held on by red grass. This is a *tikwalo*, 'male gourd'. This long, thin gourd, varying in colour from yellow to red, is the obligatory vessel for offerings to the ancestors.[35]

There seems no need here to talk of either male or female containers as 'being' or 'symbolising' or 'representing' penis, vagina or sexuality (fig. 34). They are clearly structured by this opposition and motivated with reference to it. While symbolism may be said at times to 'express' meanings and be 'about' certain things, it is futile to suggest that everything has meaning or that structure and meaning are the same thing.[36] The touchstone of symbolicity is motivation, either external or internal. Whether this builds to a level where we may talk of propositions is an empirical matter for each culture, and to be judged according to its yield as a descriptive model. (The fatuity of propositional meanings such as those given by Radcliffe-Brownian symbolic analyses, i.e. notions of 'expressing

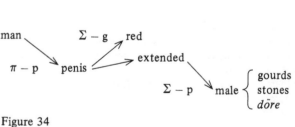

Figure 34

social value' etc., warns us that this method may be totally circular and unrewarding.) It is in the nature of symbolic systems to invoke huge redundancy and motivate gratuitously.[37] An opposition that may be important in one area is extended gratuitously until we may wish to regard it as a 'theme' of that culture. We should thus feel free to dismiss the complexities of fig. 34 in favour of a looser, more general notion of the thematic value of the male/female opposition as both a linguistic device and — not at all the same thing — a mechanism of cultural symbolism. We shall see later that there are other such 'themes' in Dowayoland, the richest being that of 'heads' that we have already alluded to. It is now time to return to the development of this theme via the problem of water.

5   Water and fertility

Myth 2

There was an old mountain man. As he journeyed, he came across many women fishing at a dam. They took the fish out of the water and put them in their calabashes. The old man asked them for some but they refused and gave him nothing. He went off and took remedies from his skin bag. He put on a leopard skin and shook himself. He became a leopard. He sat down on a flat stone behind the women and roared. The women screamed and fled naked. The old man took the fish. This happened long ago. It is finished.

This was a story told me by various people at Kpan to explain the rain-chief's ability to change into a leopard. We see a common armature with Myth 1 (fig. 35) so that we can see that it is structured at least to that degree.

Myth 1 explains the distinction between leopards and 'leopard's sons' and thus between circumcisers and the clowns and candidates who adopt ritual roles with them. Myth 2 explains the similarity between leopards and rainchiefs, the relative status of hunting and fishing, and possibly the opposition between static and moving water.

Fishing is divided between the sexes. Men fish with traps and spears i.e. the same means as used in hunting. It is considered an occupation worthy only of boys and poor men.[38] Women fish by building a barrage across the river and picking up the stranded fish, or by emptying the pools left as the rivers dry up after the end of the rains. Alternatively they may use poison. This means may be used together with a barrage and kills the fish by suffocation. Previously, a certain tree-bark was used. Nowadays, Dowayos

| A mountain leopard | | roared | at his children |
| A leopard/mountain man | | | at women |

| some of whom | fled | losing the chance to be leopards. |
| all of whom | | losing their catch to a leopard. |

Figure 35

use the pesticide Landrine that they get from cotton growers. A boy takes
two handfuls and jumps into the water backwards, flailing about 'like a
dying fish'. Another boy fires an arrow into the water beside him and he
floats on the water. We can present this as fig. 36.

The disdain that men have for fishing aligns it with female pursuits,
while the simulated 'hunting' of poisoned fish recognises its closeness to
male pursuits. When discussing the division of labour, Dowayo men refer
to fishing as 'women's hunting'. There is no suggestion that poison would
not work without the participation of uncircumcised boys but it would be
'bad' (*berge*). Men are often banned entirely from female fishing parties on
the grounds that women may strip naked.

Certain other facts must be noted here to discern the structuring of this
area. Firstly, men class the smell of women and fish together. I have
already pointed out that Dowayos often invoke smell as the explanatory
feature in mechanistic explanations. Traditional Dowayo men (Mango
area) still refuse to eat fish on grounds of its similarity to the female organ.
It will be recalled that the most appalling thing an ordinary Dowayo could
visualise would be for the vagina to get involved in his food. Many
Dowayos are dubious about eggs for similar reasons.

Secondly, human death is inimical to waterholes. After a death in a
village, the waterholes must be treated to prevent them drying up. In the
case of a woman this involves driving a millet stalk into the water.[39]

There is an ill-formulated but prevalent belief that, in some sense, rainfall makes women pregnant. This is current throughout much of West
Africa and by no means limited to Dowayos.[40]

It should be remarked that it is the rainchief especially who has the
proper *zepto* plant for curing male impotence. Taking all this in conjunc-
tion with fig. 7 (p. 15), we begin to glimpse the outlines of a second structure as in fig. 37. It is unnecessary to show how well this fits with the view
of woman as an unflawed vessel that has been presented in the exposition
of Dowayo beliefs *re* conception (above). Instead it is time to analyse the
relations between human and agrarian fertility in general.

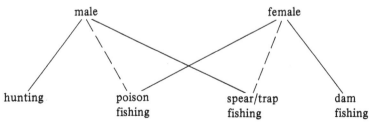

Figure 36

Dowayos have no general word for 'plants'. They divide this category into 'trees' (*tēeyoh*), 'grass' (*hētoh*), 'fruit' (*humle*) and 'leaves' (*kpase*). They accept as a general principle that all plants exist in both male and female but are vague in the extreme about the importance of sex and the manner of procreation. One very rapidly gets down to the level of: 'We do not know, we have not seen.' They accept as a general principle that all fruit-bearing plants are female, but apart from this criterion, they have no way of determining the sex of a tree.

The fertility of plants is maintained by means of certain stones contained in pots (fig. 38). These are in the possession of the rainchiefs and the Masters of the Earth at Daksidongo. At Kpan and Mango fertility cults are referred to as *donyo* (which I take to be the same word as 'cooking pot'). At Daksidongo, they are called *gbaame*. All the men involved sum up their activities as *we gepsik heptbo* 'we repair/fix/order the land'.

Each area goes about its business in a somewhat different fashion.

rainfall : retained water : : sperm : fertilisation

Figure 37

Figure 38

At Kpan, the stones are kept either under the rainchief's granary or with the skulls on the mountain of *Waaduufi*. The determining factor is the rain-stones. At the height of the rainy season, the Old Man of Kpan frequently has need of these and the plant-stones are kept in the same place. Only the millet-stones are in physical contact with the rain-stones, but there are stones for millet, peanuts, yams, taro, in fact for all the cultivated plants. Treatment is according to the simplest principles of external motivation e.g. hens' eggs are broken on the millet-stones 'so the millet will grow big like an egg', goat's horns are soaked in water and the gombo-stones washed with it so that the gombo will grow to the same shape as the horn. Various sorts of grass are also involved. In August, before anyone can begin to cut grass for weaving mats or roofs, a plait of *helle* (from which brooms are also made) is woven and hung on the skull-house roof, the *wagle* and the roofs of the chief's huts. This is practised by most skull-houses and not just at Kpan. At Kpan, however, a second plait is added later for the two other important grasses *sole* and *gbohgle*. The first time that taro and gombo are eaten, they are cooked alone on the fire in the public circle in the early morning. The men go to the skull-house and weave the plait of *gbohgle* and *sole* and hang it up there and in the village. Women and children remain in the huts in total silence. The men then go and light the first bush fire of the year at *Waaduufi*. Henceforth any man may light a fire to clear grass. All the people now eat the new crops and fling the remains on the *wagle*. Henceforth this year's crops may be eaten.

The Dowayos distinguish a number of forms of millet. Foremost amongst them all, however, is 'bird-millet', the small, highland *fonio* that makes the strongest beer. All beer offered to the ancestors is ideally made from this millet. The first millet of the year, like all the crops mentioned so far, must be offered by another person. It is spat out three times and the fourth time swallowed.[41] In all these 'first fruit' ceremonies, the vegetable is prepared with the minimum of cuisine, often just roasted directly on the fire.

At Mango, the remedies for millet are applied directly to the stones in the rain-pots in the bush. Blood of a black chicken has already been applied to start the rainy season. Then the blood of a black goat is added. The first *fonio* to ripen is crushed and fermented and thrown on the stones; these are then washed in water and wiped dry and the rainy season is over. All the other millet will ripen. The empty stalks (*tohtzuule*) 'the heads of the millet' are hung on the *wagle*.

The first bush-fire of the year is started at the skull-house. The first gombo is cooked in the public space on the same day. After this, it must always be cooked inside a hut, like all other food in the rainchief's village, for the inhabitants must never ingest rain directly. The remains of the meal are flung on the *wagle*. Later in the year, *helle* grass will be hung on the same spot, woven together with other fruits that come into season at that time.

At Daksidongo, there are also round stones, governing the fertility of millet. They are kept in a pot in the mountain skull-house. The Masters of the Earth dress up in *tutugyo* (lianas worn by women at other festivals) and go together to the skull-house. They smear the stones with water and millet-flour, and fling more on the threshold of the hut. They do the same to a special large stone on the mountain which is called *Nohlukoh* 'big (female) hut'. All go to the *wagle* where they smear themselves with oil and hang up their leaves. By now it is dark and all the people from the village are shut up in their huts. The Masters of the Earth sleep alone, naked, in their huts. Should they encounter a stranger, they must not speak to him. He would die. At the beginning of this period, big crosses of *gbohgle* grass are placed about the fields under stones.

At the beginning of the rains, various herbal remedies are placed under two lines of stones across the road on either side of the village. These are described as a 'barrier against famine' and remedies will be placed under them for any festival in the village, to prevent fights, keep away gendarmes, etc.

A peculiarity of Daksidongo is 'shouting at the *wagle*'. This occurs when the millet is about to form seeds. The organisers go to the *wagle* in the early morning and shout: 'Do not let the plant *bōk* deceive you!' *Bōk* is a wild, millet-like plant that gives no fruit. This act ensures that the fields indeed produce millet not *bōk*. *Yoboh* beans and borassus fruit must also be hung on the *wagle* before being eaten each year, otherwise scorpions will be attracted to the village by their smell.[42]

To see how all this fits, we must return to fig. 25 (p. 35). I set up a distinction between stones (the permanent pool) and skulls (the individual dead). This, I suggested, is replaced in the case of humans by the distinction post-*wagle* and pre-*wagle*. In the case of rainchiefs there is a further complication. At Mango, heads are replaced by jars and there is no skull-ceremony to place these on the *wagle*. The skull-house here contains, not human skulls, but the pots and stones that control rainfall. At Kpan, there is also no ceremony and skulls are amalgamated with stones by being buried on the stone mountain called *Waaduufi* which, it will be recalled, means 'the soft spot on top of a boy's head'. We now learn that this is the stone involved in both rainfall and millet ripening, as are the pots in the transformed skull-house at Mango. I think it is clear that in these two locations millet, rainfall, and human fertility have coalesced. We can show the processes of neutralisation as in figs. 40 and 41. Note that millet is left outside the neutralisation on one side of the diagram (fig. 40). It is this that turns up as the 'heads of the millet' hung up each year on the *wagle*.

At Kpan, the coalescence of the 'stone' end is fairly complete. The rain-stone on the top of *Waaɗuufi* controls the fertility of millet and rain. It is here that the skulls of rainchiefs are physically buried and the whole is a stone mountain with a name evoking skulls.

On the 'skull' end of the diagram, as before, coalescence is less complete. Once more 'heads'[43] of millet are attached to the *wagle*, bringing together human and agrarian. But rainfall is not represented there. In fact, as will be remembered, this is achieved by the mobile stones that move into and out of the village together with the millet stones. This now provides a filler for the empty slot for Kpan in fig. 25. By the redundant processes that we are coming to expect, these neutralisations are made in other ways at Kpan. It will be recalled that the rain- and millet-stones are stored in the granary of the rainchief. This, of course, is where a man stores his grain and the ongoing link between harvests, his seed. At the end of a harvest, a Dowayo 'true cultivator' retains several of the finest stalks of millet unthreshed, i.e. their 'heads' are still attached. These should be placed first of all in the granary and sown first next year. During this time, they will be kept in intimate contact with a man's 'seed bag' (*dōotsaayo*). These are possessed by many men concerned to cultivate well and contain remedies to ensure good harvests. I was able to examine the contents (fig. 42) of a number of these while in Dowayoland. They contain stones, horns, cocks' eggs,[44] boas' heads and their stony excrement, and hardened

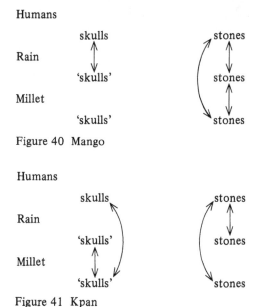

Humans

Rain

Millet

Figure 40 Mango

Humans

Rain

Millet

Figure 41 Kpan

resin of trees, i.e. the stony, lumpy, hard parts of nature. They are contained in a white liana bag inside which the unthreshed seed millet may also be placed. The physical collocation of all these elements, once more, serves to bracket them together.

Many of these seed bags also contain an iron ring. This is to ensure that the good effects of the remedies are confined to a man's own fields. This provides a link with the rainmaker's mobile 'rain-kit' which enables him to cause localised downpours within the wider phenomenon of the rainy season. Once again, this is heavily motivated externally. It consists of a goat horn containing a modern blue child's marble ('the ancestors gave it many thousands of years ago') which attracts dark, swirling clouds; wool from a ram to bring fluffy clouds; a ring to localise effects. Runny grease is wiped onto the stone and rain will fall.[45] The Old Man of Kpan always carries this with him in the wet season so that he can cause short downpours at festivals, etc. The organisers then bring him beer to make it stop.

It must be stressed that here I am only dealing with two skull-houses. There are several hundred houses in Dowayoland which reproduce various parts of the *donyo/gbaame* complex together with their own elaborations. I choose these only because they are universally recognised by Dowayos

Figure 42

as being in the *heptzuulyaayo* 'earth-head-man' class which is definitive of 'correctness'.

The *gbaame* at Daksidongo is less complex because rainfall is not involved here. Rainfall in this area is controlled by the Old Man of Kpan. The two-category of 'skulls' versus 'stones' seems, however, to hold. Flour is put on the stones in the skull-house and the stone, *Nohlukoh*. Nothing is placed on the *wagle* gate. It is as if the system has been laterally displaced as in fig. 43.

The term *Nohlukoh* 'old (female) hut' evokes that of *Waaduufi* 'the top of the boy's head'. Whereas one links the whole human/animal/agrarian fertility/rainfall complex, the latter is concerned only with humans, animals and fields.

We already saw the link between skulls/pots/huts when considering the problem of the hut with the unbeaten floor. I pointed out at the time that huts also had 'heads' and 'bellies'. While the binary contrast between what I have termed the 'skull' end and the 'stone' end of figs. 25, 40, 41 and 43 structures this area, the opposition is less firmly adhered to on the margins. Thus, the heads of goats, sheep etc. are simply thrown away as of no importance, although stones for these beasts exist. Within the domain of domesticated animals, cattle are pre-eminent, in much the same way that *fonio* millet is within the plant domain. Similarly, there are no actual stones for the various sorts of grass that are hung on the *wagle* (*gbohgle*, *sole*, *helle*): these are instead put on the 'head' of a man's hut and more particularly on the hut of the 'headman' (Dowayos have the same usage as ourselves: 'head-man' *zuulyaayo*). Once again, redundancy takes over and we end up with the reduplication of fig. 44. The rainchief's head will be shaved on the same day that the mountain 'Boy's Head' is cleaned by burning.

Once again Daksidongo is different. The fact that we find here the *gbohgle* grass on the fields under a rock shows the same displacement as fig. 43, i.e. towards the 'stone' end. This is also the place to point out that the granaries of the Dowayos are unique in that the roofs are made of *gbohgle* grass except around the Daksidongo area where I have seen them

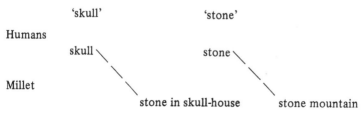

Figure 43 Daksidongo

roofed with borassus palm leaves.[46] This is also the area where the red 'hat' of *gbohgle* grass called *dōrzuule 'dōre* head' is found, during the skull-festival. As pointed out above, the *dōre* is for humans what the *wagle* is for cattle. Here too, then, we find a displacement. Instead of *gbohgle* being permanently in 'skull' position over the granary it is temporarily in 'skull' position on the 'human *wagle*' during a 'skull' period.

As regards the other plants that may be thrown on the *wagle* – gombo, borassus, yams etc. – it is often a matter of dispute whether or not stones exist separately for these. Every Dowayo gives a separate list for those that do and do not have stones, and locates them differently. We note that these fruits have one point in common, their 'head-like' quality. That this is so can be seen from the externally motivated remedies I collected in various areas of Dowayoland (see above, 'gombo' and 'millet'). It seems that any connection with heads may provide sufficient motivation for their inclusion in this omnivorous system. Thus, around the Kingle area (between Mango and Kpan) the plant *fāzuulyo* 'sticky head', used to make a head pad for carrying burdens, is affixed to roofs and the *wagle*. Whatever the variations among the numerous skull-houses of Dowayoland, we have established the basic armature and it seems probable that all 'idiolects' or even 'dialects' (if Daksidongo is typical of the area it is surrounded by) can be treated as transformations of the same structure. It is always comforting when a displacement or transformation posited in one limited area (e.g. fig. 43) turns out to be more general (as in the treatment of *gbohgle*). Such evidence is the only criterion of validation that we can apply. I have already stated that our touchstones should be measures of completeness, elegance and simplicity which, of course, can only be judged over the system as a whole. It is to be hoped that the question of the representational model of cultural symbolism posed in chapter 3 is now beginning to seem clearer. I have pointed to strong external motivation in several systems but it has always been found within a more pervasive internal structuring. Although at times structures of internal motivation, such as 'skull to human is as roof to hut', may be rephrased in terms of external motivation, i.e. 'the roof represents a skull', 'the hut is a symbol of the human body', there is a very real difference between these two forms.

It is not simply that the roof 'symbolises a skull'; it sets up a more general system that relates both to each other by a common structure. The

Head	: body	: : 'head'	: grass
		: : ('head') roof	: hut
		: : headman	: village

Figure 44

roof never ceases to be a roof, its other qualities are always available to enter into other motivations. So perhaps we should query the direction of the arrows in the diagrams of chapter 4, replacing them with two-way traffic. It seems reasonable to point the arrows in a single direction only when the description gains something from it. Thus, in figs. 40 and 41, the arrows go both ways. In later chapters, we shall deal with processes that involve sequential ordering, where it makes a great difference whether we derive A from B or B from A. The great weakness of external motivation, representational symbolic interpretations, is their inherent *ad hoc* nature. The role that representational symbolism may be held to play in the interpretation of culture remains to be established by trading off its obvious explanatory power against this fundamental weakness. Such a decision involves judgments about the essential nature of culture and, by implication, the human unconscious, that we may feel temporarily unequipped to make.

Before facing such complexities, let us continue to develop the map of Dowayo structures that has been begun. As has been noted (figs. 40 and 41) heads are associated with rainfall and fertility. We have already looked at some of the relations that structure this, but there remain more to be teased out. We start with Myth 3 which deals with the origin of circumcision.

6 *Tarniisnohgbarklele:* 'the place where the old Fulani woman was beaten to death'

Myth 3

An old Fulani woman had a son. He was ill. He had run in the *silkoh* grass and cut himself. His penis swelled up and was full of pus. She took a knife and cut so the child was cured. The penis became beautiful. She cut her second son. One day she went for a walk through a Dowayo village and the Dowayos saw it was good. They took circumcision and beat her to death. That was how it started because Dowayos did not know circumcision. They forbade women to see it. But Fulani women can see it. It is finished.

The killing of the old Fulani woman is re-enacted on several occasions. At the end of the 'sticking of the bow' rites where a man's bow is fixed behind the skull-house, his brothers, brothers of circumcision and the clown assemble, naked except for penis sheaths, before the *dōre*. The clown puts on leaves and adopts the high-pitched, bad-tempered tone of an old woman. At the back he wears a long tail of borassus leaves that trail along the ground. On his head he carries a basket. His 'husband' is with him urging him along. Other men crouch down with sticks.

'What are those black things in the road?' asks the old woman.

'It is nothing. They are cattle.'

'I am frightened, it's getting dark.'

'There's no need to be frightened. I have my bow.'

The couple pass three times between the men. On the fourth time, the men leap up with a cry and beat the 'tail' with their sticks. This may be seen by men only. Even boys are excluded. The whole operation is carried out with the sense of wicked fun that characterises all-male events. (See Appendix III (f), II (f).)

The transvestite takes full advantage of opportunities to bend down and expose himself to spectators like a careless woman. This performance is immediately preceded by the miming of circumcision in the bush by the same actors.

Just before the newly circumcised boys return to the village, they too enact the same indigenous 'play' in the bush. The borassus 'tail' is buried under a pile of stones near the circumcision grove. The action occurs

60

beneath a thorn tree, hence its full name *Tarekopse* 'Fulani thorn'. We
have already encountered this (p. 28) as the tree that makes jars water-
proof and seals floors. Its appropriateness becomes clear from the importance of the open/closed opposition we looked at before.

A millet stick is pushed into the stones,[47] and the basket and a red
Fulani fez are attached to the top. The place is called *Tarniisnohgbarklele*
'the place where the old Fulani woman was beaten to death'. Sometimes a
blue and a white robe are draped from the sticks. This raises a problem in
the sex assigned to the 'victim', since Fulani women − so far as I am aware
− wear neither the red fez nor robes of this sort but a loose, sari-type
dress. When confronted with this problem, Dowayos either shrug it off or
suggest that *old* Fulani women did, in the past, wear these clothes when
past childbearing.

In the internecine struggles between the Fulani and the Dowayos, when
a Fulani was killed he would be buried under such a pile of stones. The
same would happen to a Dowayo outsider who was killed in a hostile
village.

At the end of the skull-ceremony, the organiser climbs onto the *wagle*
and shouts: 'I have organised this skull-festival and circumcised these men.
If it were not for the White Man (i.e. the interference of central government) I would have killed a man.'

Questioning on this matter is greeted with strong denials that such a
statement is to be taken at its face value. Some men explained that the
reference was to the fights that occurred between drunken men. Others
said that it was 'play' (*dangoh*). Very old men agreed that it sometimes
happened, very young Christians claimed that wicked pagan Dowayos used
to crucify men on the *dōre* 'like Jesus'. The victim was apparently a willing
participant and much honoured by the choice. Christian Dowayos have
assimilated the *dōre* to the cross (fig. 45). Old Dowayos who came to trust
me after some two years' acquaintance told a different tale. For the skull-
festival a human should, indeed, be killed. Clearly, it was impossible to
arrange this on the actual day of the festival but it should happen while
the festival was being organised. The normal method was to ambush an
outsider, Dowayo or Fulani, and kill him. The means of death was
unimportant. The killers would be the brothers or brothers of circumcision
of the man for whom the festival was being held. The victim could be of
either sex but would be dressed, after death, in a red Fulani hat. It should
be noted that this proceeding would not necessarily involve great loss of
life since many lesser men would associate themselves with the skull-
festival of a rich man. One death would thus be made to serve for many.

The important point to note for the purposes of interpretation is that
the head of the victim would be removed and pounded to pieces. Burial
would be under a pile of stones in the bush. Old mountain Dowayos can

still identify stones marking men killed in their grandfathers' time. The
men would then return to the village, set up a new *dōre* and sing the
battle-song as they circled it.

This clearly introduces a new and important variation into fig. 25.
Human death is now tacitly divided into two forms, 'domestic death'
aligned with cattle, and 'violent death' aligned with hunting, the wild, and
the leopard. I present this information in fig. 46. The *dōre* spatially, and
the leopard metaphysically, are the points of intersection of nature and
culture. While the head of the victim is utterly destroyed, the head of the

Figure 45

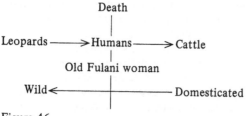

Figure 46

leopard is preserved and placed on the *dōre*, then on the *wagle* during the skull-festival. There is thus a movement from violent to domesticated death.

For the purposes of this interpretation, it is relatively unimportant whether we trust the shaky memories of old men with their tales of violent death, or the biased views of young Christians who speak of the immolation of a willing victim. In one, as in the other, we see the domestication of death, at the *wagle*, while the *dōre* emphasises man as killer.

But if death is domesticated in one respect, there is a corresponding shift in the other direction in the categorisation of agriculture. The death-drum, beaten at the death of a human, contains the 'neck' of a leopard (as if the head had been destroyed after the fashion of human victims and wild beasts) housed in the vessel in which millet is crushed and covered with the skin of the wild buffalo.

This interesting collocation suggests that we might with profit consider other examples of the coalescence of human and agricultural matters that may shed light on it.

For example, the opposition between blacksmith and Dowayo that is maintained in the sexual domain extends to agriculture as well. A blacksmith's fields must be separated from those of his neighbours by a strip of uncleared bush. He may pass freely over the fields of others until seed has been sown. Then he may not enter. If threshed millet is being transported to or from the fields, he must swiftly remove himself from the roadway and not speak to the man carrying it. Specifically forbidden is the act of approaching a 'true cultivator's' granary. Women, too, should not approach or enter the fields of a 'true cultivator'. The centre of agrarian fertility, a man's seed-bag, is also totally forbidden to women. The phallic potential of a tubular granary full of seed parallels that of the blacksmith's bellows. This would seem once again to be a simple case of 'representational symbolism' but we should be alert by now to the internal structuring of the whole.

The male blacksmith's bellows causes the pollution disease (*zaase*), as we saw above. This is linked with the female potter's pollution, but where is this centred? In fact, the area of particular danger is the fire where the pots are baked. The ashes of this cause instant *zaase*. Anything the blacksmiths want to leave in a place safe from theft, they put in the ashes, just as a 'true cultivator' puts them in his granary. So we have a series:

bellows : potter's fire : : penis[48] : womb : : granary : *x*

There is no doubt as to the identity of the missing element. The fact that the blacksmith is dangerous to threshed millet gives the answer − the threshing floor (*dangkoh*) (fig. 47).

Given the value assigned to the terms in this series, we might well imagine that dangers would be inherent in the threshing floor. Indeed, this is the case. A pregnant woman is particularly threatened and should never set foot in the *dangkoh*, 'unless the baby is finished and moving in her'. Otherwise premature birth will result.

But there is a difficulty here. The external motivation is sufficiently strong for 'threshing floor' to be coded as a female element. What happens to a true cultivator's *dangkoh*? This element would be simultaneously coded male/female. We could imagine several ways in which this could be dealt with. Uncircumcised boys, as we shall see later, are male/female; we could imagine a solution whereby they would be charged with threshing. Likewise, the transvestite comedians are male/female. They could be involved. In fact, the Dowayos use another element coded in the same fashion — *Tarniisnohgbarklele* — 'the place where the old Fulani woman was beaten to death'.

The threshing floor is made in a circular depression in the field. Its floor is sealed with *tarekupse* or gombo and given a coat of cattle excrement that hardens in the sun. For ordinary Dowayos, anyone may help in the threshing. It is only the 'true cultivators' who are subject to restrictions. Normally their threshing is done at night when there are fewer people about. Women should not be present at all. If they *are* allowed in the area,

Figure 47

it is only to carry away the grain. They must not witness the threshing, nor step in the hollow. The stalks of millet are heaped up, in the centre, with various remedies against witchcraft, e.g. *nyomptare* (note 15). The men sing the *yaako* circumcision song that is intoned when a boy is cut. The sticks they use should be of *gōkoh* wood like those carried by circumcision candidates. The stick is swung up and over the head with the right arm. Here the left hand grips it too, and it is swung down two-handed onto the millet. The beaters move one pace clockwise and beat again. At the end of the operation, the owner must carry the first millet into his compound in a basket on his head. A millet stick is pushed into it and on top a red hat. In other words, the threshing of a 'true cultivator's' millet is depicted in terms of the beating to death of the old Fulani woman.

In chapter 3, I looked at some aspects of riddles and pointed out that they rarely have unique solutions. If we rephrase the 'beating to death of the old Fulani woman' as a riddle, it runs:

What (male) female death leads to the birth of true males?

Answer: The beating to death of the old Fulani woman, the threshing of a 'true cultivator's' female millet to give male seed, the circumcision of boys to give men.

We see here how the strangely male dress of the old Fulani woman fits into a system of classes marked simultaneously male/female.

Millet itself is associated with the whole series of female changes over time. Thus we find that when a girl menstruates for the first time she is obliged to be shut up in the grinding house for three days.[49] We have seen that the threshing operation is clearly associated with imminent childbirth. Germinated millet (beer) is one category of gifts made to the ancestors. We can present this as fig. 48.

To this we may add one more. Just as it is believed that adultery is inimical to bovine and human fertility, so it has terrible consequences for the fields. A woman who commits adultery will have her fields completely destroyed by monkeys and cattle which will be irresistibly attracted by the smell. So, ravaged millet correlates with adultery.

We might expect to find another male plant set up in opposition to the heavily 'female' millet, and indeed we do — yams. Dowayos are, as stated, very vague about plant sexuality. However, they declare one particular yam *taabmaatoh* ('the yam of the bow') to be male.[50] It is planted around

Human	copulation	affinity	menstruation	circumcision /birth	death
Millet	planting	germination	grinding	threshing	fermentation

Figure 48

the shelter behind the cattle-park in which the bodies of dead men are housed before burial. This is an area forbidden to women. Neither they nor uncircumcised boys may eat this yam. During the skull-festival, this yam is dug up and wrapped up with the dead man's bow in burial cloth. The man's brother of circumcision carries the bundle and dances, accompanied by the other circumcised men from the bush, to the *dōre* waving weapons while the uncircumcised seek to snatch it from them. They are repulsed, and the bundle is placed on the *wagle*, the yam being later planted under the dead men's shelter. After circumcision, it is this yam[51] that is given to a boy to eat, by his sponsor. It is cooked in the public space in a large pot and placed between his legs. He bites off three pieces from the uncut yam, spitting to either side alternately, and without touching the yam with his hands. The fourth bite, he may swallow. It is hard not to be simply overwhelmed by the external symbolism of this plant. It is long, penis-shaped and, when cut or peeled, exudes a white liquid smelling strongly of male sexual fluid. This yam may not be cut with a knife. Women must avert their eyes as the *taabmaatoh* passes. Quite obviously male sexuality is involved but less in the form of an extended correlation between two series than is the case with 'female' millet. The natural basis of the distinction probably lies in the fact that yams proliferate without seed. The normal means of propagation is simply to cut a section of the root or sucker and push it in the ground. We should note the association with death — the dead men's shelter,[52] the skull-festival, the *wagle*, the man's bow. Just as the collapse of the human/rain/agriculture area leads to notions that we may express as the association of rainfall and skull, rainfall and human fertility, in short the association of death and fertility in a single category, so the opposition between yams and millet within the *Tarniisnohgbarklele* complex justifies the association of male sexuality and violent death that is manifested in the bow bundle. I attempt to present this in fig. 49. Such associational nodes are not uncommon in anthropological writings (see, for example, Ardener 1970). Often they will structure whole areas of behaviour but remain difficult to motivate. In the present case, it can be seen how such an associational group results from the internal structure of the rest of the system.

It would be a matter of considerable interest to know how far the somewhat loose and uneasy expressions of associational phraseology may be more generally replaced by descriptions in terms of internal motivation.

It is noteworthy that we seem here to be approaching an area where we might wish to begin to talk of 'meaning' and express the burthen of Dowayo symbolism in propositions phrased in quite general and abstract terms. As regards the assemblage of paraphernalia before the *dōre* and *wagle* at the skull-festival, we could construct a message of the form, 'the Dowayos, in their cultural symbolism, recognise that death is an integral

part of life and necessary for its continuation on another plane'. Or 'the
Dowayos realise that life and death occur in various modes whose underlying unity finds expression in the skull-ceremony'.

Of course, any categorisation can be rephrased as a proposition. Even
the weakest form of internal motivation, the constant recombining of the
same elements in different patterns, could be expressed as, 'in their symbolism, the Dowayos recognise the essential unity within diversity of life'.
The problem with this, as with external motivation, lies in its surplus
generativity. Abstractly formulated principles and simple equations would
account for cases that do not occur. If pots were equated with wombs why
does not a Dowayo woman believe that she will be infertile if she drops
her pot and breaks it? Such a belief would have been 'explained' in
advance; it unfortunately does not occur. As for 'unity within diversity' it
is quite incapable of accounting for unique elements that *do* occur.

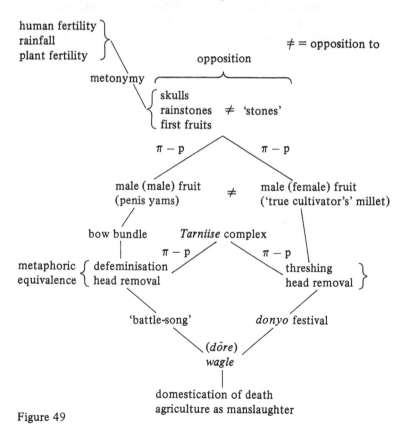

Figure 49

The situation is not dissimilar to that encountered by linguists at the lowest levels of morphology. When compiling their lexicons, linguists must decide to what degree elements are to be generated by process and to what degree they are to be simply listed. For example, they might wish to set up a general rule of suffixation whereby *-able* could be affixed to verb forms to give *wearable, washable*, etc. As it stands, however, it also gives forms such as *getable, *electable which are potentially rather than actually part of the language. The position can be improved by the introduction of relevance restrictions like those suggested in chapter 4 but it is difficult to see how this technique could apply to general abstract statements. The normal linguistic resource would be to list exceptions. In cultural symbolism it is not even clear what would have to be included in such a list, since we almost totally lack techniques by which cultural symbolism can be formalised. In the absence of prior formalisation, it is nonsense even to speak of rule-following or rule-breaking. There exists, of course, the possibility that the generativeness of our models could be preserved by a shift in time depth, that models would tend to generalise rules over time and that we could study how shifts in one area will affect other parts.

This problem is far from being a new one. The attempt to portray 'magic' as failed science has shattered largely because of this difficulty. Thematic models of interpretation such as Llewellyn and Hoebel (1941) and Zamora (1971) have all foundered on the same rock. It works well enough as a 'receiver's model', i.e. given that the Dowayos do such and such we can see how they might be able to interpret it as in keeping with established themes. We cannot, however, explain why on earth they should select such a perverse means of making propositional statements in the first place. It is far from clear that it is legitimate to call such themes 'meaning' anyway. They are in the nature of presuppositions (Cooper 1974) rather than communication itself.

A second way in which the anthropologist might be tempted to extend his interpretations into the domain of general propositions is to see rituals such as the skull-ceremony as logically ranking not themes of moral content but whole models of the world. In this case, the skull-ceremony would express the triumph of life over death in the incorporation of the myth-derived model of killing into the vegetation-derived model of reincarnation. It is far from clear that this is justified. The Dowayo ceremony seems simply to juxtapose all elements on the grounds of their inherent similarity and then move on without any obvious drawing of conclusions.

On the whole, Dowayo symbolic activity seems to concern itself more with working out chains of linkage that shift the arbitrary to the motivated, to bring together crucial points in the existence of humans in their wild and domesticated aspects, plants and the instruments of rainfall.

For the moment, we would be wise to admit that thematic approaches concentrate on the ways in which a receiver interprets a product rather than with the manner in which it is produced and that such general principles must therefore be regarded with about as much respect as we accord literary themes in the analysis of actual works. In culture, as in literature, the degree to which an object of analysis is 'about' something may be expected to vary according to all manner of conditions.

7 'It is only thanks to me that you were circumcised'

Thus far, we have looked at some of the simpler processes at work in culture, the punctuation into domains, themes, representational symbolism and basic forms of process relating one classification to another. The study of liminality involves a higher level of analysis, in that the marker 'liminality' already requires a preliminary categorisation before it can enter into other systems.

Liminality is portrayed in Dowayo culture above all in the classification of relationships. Kinship relations are firmly affective. Parents are warm and affectionate but sexuality must never be mentioned before mother or sister. Parents-in-law are treated with great respect. Sexuality is never to be mentioned.[53] One should never look them directly in the face when speaking to them. A woman should adopt 'respect posture' (on knees, hands over genitals, face averted) when speaking to her husband's father, as should a man when speaking to his wife's mother. A man has a special relationship with his nephew or niece. They are expected to be mutually free and intimate. They may make free with each other's possessions. The relationship is of great ceremonial importance.

Quite distinct from these links are another series of relationships. In life a man acquires a number of 'brothers of circumcision', men who underwent circumcision in the same year as himself. Clearly, he cannot know every single man who was circumcised that year, especially if they are from the other end of Dowayoland. Out of this group, therefore, he will select some small number with whom he has regular contacts and these will become 'his' brothers of circumcision. Similarly, a woman acquires 'sisters of circumcision' who began menstruating in the same year as herself. The relationship between such persons is what is normally termed a 'joking relationship'. Whenever a man happens upon his brother of circumcision, he will make insulting remarks to him. Insults normally centre on circumcision itself. A favourite is: 'It is only thanks to me that you were circumcised.' By this, he means that the speaker's father made all the arrangements with the circumcisers and assumed all the responsibility and expenditure involved, while the other man's father merely associated himself with these arrangements later. Such is the mark of a poor man. Such men are expected to play tricks on each other and help themselves freely to each other's beer and tobacco. At the funeral of a brother of circumcision, a man may steal the body, flinging it into a stream or hiding it until payment is made. At the funeral of a poor man, brothers of circumcision mock the dead mercilessly, bringing 'gifts of millet' in the form of baskets of ashes or skinning a mouse and dancing with its skin as one would with the hides of slaughtered cattle. It is the brothers of circumcision who must spit on the women and goods of a dead man to release them for the use of others, and it is they who dispose of his most dangerous and personal possessions after death.

There is another class of persons with whom one has similar relations. These are the *duuse*. Dowayos are far from clear how to classify them. Some maintain that they are 'like relatives' (*an doohdmihiiya*), others that they are 'affines' (*gonmihiiya*), others still that they are neither. They are addressed as *yaa* ('grandfather'), a term used to all old men, or *naa* ('grandmother'), used to all old women. Expressed biologically, the term refers to a man (or woman) removed by at least three generations with whom I have at least one affinal linkage as a wife-taker/-giver. Thus it covers MoFaFa, FaMoFa, MoMoFa, FaFaMo, FaMoMo, MoFaMo, MoMoMo. What is important is that there should be a common relative at the great-grandfather level and at least one female linkage between. Thus, my agnatic great-grandfather is not a *duuse*, nor any named relative at all. Dowayo very firmly cut off kinship at the grandfather level. *Duuse* are theoretically marriageable and the term will be used of their sons and daughters too. They belong to different skull-houses from me. In the case of marriage the affective aspects of that relationship override those of the *duuse* relationship. Dowayos readily admit that they cannot know who is a *duuse*, especially with the complications introduced by frequent divorce and polygamy. As with brothers of circumcision, therefore, one is given not so much a finite number of *duuse* as a vast number of potential *duuse* who will be recognised as such or not according to all manner of local contingencies, such as residence, personal empathy, suitability of mutual age, etc. It will be clear from this that *duuse* may show great disparity of age or be broadly contemporaries. In their ceremonial duties, notably carrying the skulls of the dead, *duuse* are always old men. It is generally believed that carrying the skulls of the dead at a skull-festival will entail the death of that particular *duuse* within a few years. Only very old men may therefore be prevailed upon to undertake it and it is only required that they take the first few shaky steps before a younger man, not necessarily in the *duuse* relationship, takes over. There is, moreover, the consideration that contemporary *duuse* will tend to be brothers of circumcision. It is only in specific references to circumcision that the latter relationship tends to be different. The same freedom is taken as regards property and insult between *duuse* as between brothers of circumcision. The approach of *duuse*, especially in groups, is greeted with resigned trepidation. Although Dowayos frequently become exasperated at the excesses of *duuse*, this is considered reprehensible and others will intervene to establish peace between quarrelling *duuse*.

Here, then, we have two classes with whom a man is in the position of being obliged to suffer permanent insult. There is a third class, however, who are temporally defined – the clowns. If we have been previously concerned with the different models by which to understand Dowayo symbolism, we must now also consider genres of interaction within the culture. Dowayos have no word that we can translate as 'ritual' or 'ceremonial'. The native term is very wide. *Māako* covers 'custom', 'habit', 'festival', 'culture'. Festivals, however, are clearly set off in time and space. At Daksidongo, for example, special remedies are placed under the lines of stones across the road and mark it off from the non-ritual area. Special regulations about the areas closed to women, about sexual intercourse and dress and food, apply. To look at these festivals is by no means to limit symbolic interpretation to whales beached on the rocks of rationality. The setting off of these areas by the Dowayos themselves merely suggests that we should consider them all as a whole. It is at these periods that the clowns operate.

In principle, each skull-house has a sorcerer (*yaayo*) who may be either a fast sorcerer (*yaaseehsoyo*), rushing round at high speed, or a slow sorcerer (*dumnoyoh*), creeping with unearthly slowness. Blacksmith clowns are always slow. Pace marks off their actions in festivals from those of everyday life. In some areas, there may be only one sorcerer with the gourd, bell and hook that are the tokens of his office but he may lend these to other men at different skull-houses in his area. This is the case in the Kongle region and it is not impossible that such arrangements might provide an index of skull-house fission. There is a certain amount of terminological confusion. The term *yaayo* is used for all sorts of sorcerers and witches, good and bad. It is also used loosely to include the circumciser and clown. Sorcerer and clown often perform together and often I have seen a clown asked to perform a task normally allocated to the sorcerer proper, on the grounds of the infirmity of the latter. Although one's father does not have to be a clown to take up this role, one son will normally buy the right from his father.

If the sorcerer functions with the clown, then so do the brothers of circumcision. At both the 'bow-sticking' and skull-festivals, it is the brothers of circumcision and clowns who touch the dangerous personal effects of the dead and touch their skulls. Although there will be joking whenever a clown is operating, this is especially marked at skull-festivals.

Here the clowns dress up in rags or rubbish. One affected a costume made from an old fertiliser sack in blue plastic, another painted one half of his face white and left the other half black, a third wove himself a gendarme's kepi and strutted round like a gendarme who had made a great impression when visiting the village. Clowns speak in a high-pitched whine, half Fulani, half Dowayo 'to be like women'. They talk in semantic inversions. A favourite figure is the joke hunter who falls over every time he attempts to fire his bow. If he breaks his straw arrow, he cries out: 'Oh, my bow is getting stronger, my arrow better.' Obscenities are shouted. Women are not forbidden to see clowns, unless the clowns are playing their flutes, but will flee rapidly, eyes averted, across the public space where the clowns are performing. There is always the threat that a clown will expose his penis to the huge delight of onlookers. Nonsensical expressions such as 'the cunt of the beer' are screamed as they simulate copulation and emit loud farts. They jostle passers-by and attempt to mate with them. The visiting anthropologist is too good a target to miss. Clowns would frequently guy my writing of notes and 'take photographs' with a broken bowl. It is not permissible to take offence at anything a clown may do although their victims frequently repress their annoyance with difficulty and mutter curses under their breath. At a later stage of a skull-festival, it is the clowns who clean the excrement from the skulls and replace the *duuse*. The clowns take turns to perform and, when resting, squat by the side of the public circle chatting soberly and talking of the crops like venerable old men. They are either 'in role' or 'out of role'.

The liminal, marginal quality of these people seems clear. The *duuse* are kinsmen who are not kinsmen, at the very limit of social relationships. They are people with whom I have a vague feeling of kinship but to whom I cannot apply a more precise kin-term. The brothers of circumcision are people with whom a boy is pictured as dying and being reborn. The clowns are mediators between the living and the dead. They are half male, half female, half Dowayo, half Fulani, clothed but undressed, totally beyond all control on speech, gesture or behaviour. The clown, be it remembered, also wears the spotted *dōgyo* skin, associating him with the wild.

We have seen that a degree of mutual substitutability exists between these persons. They are all intimately associated with dirt and disorder. The clowns clean the skulls of excrement at the skull-festival. They are in charge of the washing, feeding and cleansing of those associated with the dead through the state of mourning (*liiloh* 'forbidden'). They handle the dead man's penis sheath, sleeping mat, bow and knife which would kill others. The *duuse* is the only one who can move the skulls on their passage from the bush to the *wagle* (i.e. from individual 'skull' towards collective 'stone'). Only the brothers of circumcision can free a man's grain and wives from the restrictions of mourning so that they become available to others again (i.e. from 'assigned' to 'disposable'). In their characters they clearly mirror their structural function as shunters from one category to another. This is at its clearest at the skull-festival which is at heart nothing but a protracted mockery of the dead.

The first thing to note is the existence of a common Dowayo gesture of insult. One of the worst insults is to take dirt with the left hand and throw it, with fingers downwards, into the face of the person to be insulted. The gesture is equally strong even if no dirt is actually flung. This is precisely the gesture used at the skull-festival when Dowayos literally fling excrement into the faces of their ancestors. A boy is only permitted to use this insult after circumcision. Should he attempt to do so earlier he will be beaten or mocked by the men. (Similarly, the greatest oath of all: *'Dang mi gere'* 'Behold my knife' is only allowed after a man is cut.)

It will be recalled that the displacement from penis to anus in the 'official version' of the circumcision ritual makes every reference to excretion a potential reference to circumcision. At the threshing of a 'true cultivator' for example, men will suggest, as a standard joke, that winnowing should be done, not by allowing the chaff to blow away in the wind, but by farting on it together. At the burial of a rich man, his brothers of circumcision all break off in the middle of the ceremony to excrete together in the bush.

The association between insult and the anus is very close. An extremely shocking gesture to make to anyone is to curl one's fingers towards one's thumb and shake and rotate them. Dowayos translate this as: 'Your anus is like this.' A man must never defecate on a grave or even sit on one. This would constitute a serious affront to the ancestors. He must never pass with his buttocks too close to the face of another or he will be shamed by the man calling out the proverbial phrase: 'Do you think because the pot is empty, it does not still smell of sauce?' There is the curious ritual on the last day of the skull-festival when a brother of circumcision of the dead man climbs onto the roof of his hut and rubs his anus against the top of the roof ('head'). (Appendix I (m).)

Given the insulting or joking nature of the association with excrement, the skull-festival is simply an elaborate insult to the dead. This process begins at the burial itself, with the jostling of the body and its treatment as a candidate for circumcision, and culminates in the assignment of the skull to its permanent position in the skull-house receiving offerings of excrement. Here, by a process of insult and mockery, it has become permanently liminal, living in the bush in a house of the village, transformed from the loving relative to the greedy, dangerous and capricious ancestor who afflicts his erstwhile kin with disease and death. This is summed up in the final remark of the son or brother who has organised the festival: 'I have circumcised these men . . . ' This is the standard insult between brothers of circumcision; the father or brother has now become a liminal figure on the margins of society, a person with whom one has a joking relationship.

The suitability of joking for performing this feat of reclassification lies simply in its implicit double nature. As Bateson (1973: 150) has pointed out with regard to play, it often consists of aggression that is not aggression, i.e. only play. All human communication occurs within brackets outside which is a sign indicating how it is to be interpreted. The sign can be changed, sometimes years later. In Dowayo culture, the sign is determined by human relations. Changing the sign requires a realignment of the relations. We can depict this as in fig. 50. This is a clear example of symbolism acting in the form of connotation (Barthes 1967: 89), based upon a prior classification of relationships. This is a clear marker that we have indeed changed the level of analysis when we deal with liminality.

There is another point. Thus far, I have spoken of 'excrement', following the literature on the subject. But, for Dowayos, this is not quite excrement. Only after excretion can one apply the word 'excrement' (*hutu*). Until that moment it is referred to as *zekoh*, the contents of stomach and intestines. Once again, a somewhat liminal material. The dissection of a bovine is strongly patterned. The head goes to the *wagle*, the forelegs to parents-in-law, carcass meat to consanguines, blood, excrement and skin to the dead, the anus to the blacksmith or dogs. We see here the vulnerability of the blacksmith, especially given the association of rain and heads, to association with excrement and death.[54] It seems that this has occurred among the neighbouring Dupa people who share many cultural traits with the Dowayos (extended circumcision, skull-cults, rainchiefs, etc.) but arranged in different patterns. Here apparently it is the blacksmith who deals with both circumcision and death. One could certainly establish a fan of transformations between the cultures of the various pagan montagnards of northern Cameroon. For Dowayos, however, even opposition with the potter-midwife has not resulted in any marked association between death and the blacksmith. Dowayos explain that no blacksmith could be

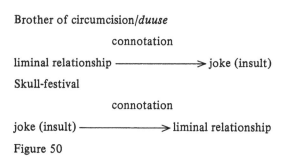

Brother of circumcision/*duuse*

connotation

liminal relationship ————————⟶ joke (insult)

Skull-festival

connotation

joke (insult) ————————⟶ liminal relationship

Figure 50

involved with a corpse of theirs because blacksmiths are *liiloh* 'forbidden' and *diibto* 'dirty'. Reverting to their favourite causal mechanism they say that contacts with blacksmiths should be limited because they smell bad. Among the Dupa, blacksmiths are concerned with death because both are unclean, whereas the Dowayos invoke this argument to deny them access to the dead.

The similarity is further indicated in the domain of food. Dowayo food consists normally of crushed, boiled millet, served in a calabash and a sauce served in a pottery vessel (small, black, with five feet). The sauce may consist of nuts, fruits, vegetables or leaves boiled with oil and sometimes spices, or alternatively of meat. Meat is either fresh or smoked. Smoked meat is meat that has been either simply cut in strips and dried in the sun or suspended in the smoke above a cooking fire. After several weeks, it exudes an odour like a corpse in a state of advanced decay.[55] It is normally prepared with either sesame or native salt and peanuts. If no smoked meat is available a sauce of salt alone may be used. Smoked meat may be eaten at any time and by any person but *must* be eaten at the end of all ceremonies concerned with the return to an unmarked ritual condition. Thus, a standard end to any festival (jar-ceremony, coming out of mourning, skull-festival) involves the participants being fed with this food, at the crossroads,[56] by the clown. They spit out three mouthfuls and eat the fourth and are then rubbed with ochre and oil and decorated with necklaces, beads, bracelets, etc.

We can phrase this in 'meaning' terms as: 'The dish of smoked meat signifies a change of ritual status', but this involves a number of confusions. We might hold that the meal does not signify the change, it effects it. We can save the appearances by invoking notions of 'performatives' (Austin 1962), which works well enough as long as we are concerned merely with changes in the definition of social reality. Once we talk about instrumental efficacy in other areas, we meet the 'magical power of words' problem (Tambiah 1968, 1973). To convert all symbolism into performative signification is simply to extend the boundaries of this last problem. I have argued that the touchstone of symbolism is the presence of the various forms of motivation, internal and external, that we have looked at in the various areas of Dowayo culture. Thus, symbolism can be consciously or unconsciously expressive of 'inner states' or presuppositions about reality, it can 'mean' and 'signify' but this is not the beginning or end of it. Truth, or falsehood, is not a sufficient criterion, neither are 'reasonableness' nor non-pragmatism. It lies rather in the diverse forms of motivation we can detect in cultural forms.

To say that the smoked-meat meal 'signifies a change of status' is, moreover, merely to convert circumstances of use into meaning[57] by a sleight of hand that adds nothing to the explanation. It is as if one should deny the necessity of writing a grammar of the English language on the grounds that it had been shown that it could be used to buy railway tickets.

The meal of smoked meat and sesame salt involves a number of categories. Smoked meat is described as *virrr* or *sōk sōk sōk*.[58] These are ideophones used to describe rottenness and decay. Salt itself is prepared from a number of plants but the most common method involves burning the millet hulls and mixing the resulting ash with goat excrement, to aid filtration, and water. The resulting liquid has a fetid, salty taste. The hulls are referred to as either 'the head of the millet' or 'millet excrement' *(toht hutu)*.

It might seem obvious that the requirement that those coming out of an unclean condition should eat smoked meat or salt rests upon an association of such constituents with notions of death and decay. However, at a funeral no such meal is eaten. The brothers of circumcision and true brothers of a man eat meat that is initially roasted directly on a fire and subsequently cooked in the three-legged pot that requires no hearth. So, we have an opposition, between the minimal cooking at a funeral, and the elaborate preparation of the smoked-meat meal. This food, be it remembered, is eaten to the accompaniment of body ornamentation and rich display. The rest of the system of food prohibitions bears this out. Newly circumcised boys are forbidden to eat salt, sesame and pimento. They must eat only bland smooth foods or their penes will be scarred. Similarly, they cannot break bones or tear tendons or gristle. If they eat meat, it is cooked directly on the fire without pot or hearth, or using the three-legged pot, after the manner of the meal eaten by brothers at a rich man's funeral.

When the boys return, after circumcision, to the village, they must eat plain yams without sauce or utensils. Likewise, first fruits, when brought to the village, are cooked directly on the fire with minimal elaboration without use of cooking hut or hearth. All such 'minimal meals' are eaten either direct from the hands of another or out of a single calabash without segregation of sauce and millet.

At a funeral, it is another meal that marks the end of this stage of a skull's career. Two brothers of the deceased place the death-drum before the *dōre*. The intestines of cattle killed for the funeral are cooked in a sesame sauce or salt and served with millet. The brothers throw this at each other across the death-drum, then everyone may eat. Although intestines may be eaten at any time by an ordinary Dowayo, we are dealing here more specifically with the large intestine, i.e. the area that is directly adjacent to the blacksmith's portion, if, indeed, it does not fall directly into his domain.[59] Sesame, it will be remembered, cannot be eaten by the rainchief and is forbidden to the newly circumcised. Dowayo children may only eat it cooked, until they are adult (after onset of menses in women, circumcision in boys), when they may eat it raw. If girls eat it raw they will never begin to menstruate. A pregnant woman who eats it will miscarry. A boy who eats it would risk circumciser's disease. If they are children of blacksmiths they may consume it in any form at any time. Once again we find the blacksmith in extreme opposition to the rainchief, with the ordinary Dowayo between the two. Moreover, it is the sauce that marks death that is his permanent prerogative. If we add to this, the information that those who are in mourning cannot eat with others, nor should they enter the compounds of others, we see that there might be a common structure to all this — blacksmiths being 'permanent mourners'.

Despite the fact that mourners are, as it were, temporary blacksmiths, this structural equivalence is not marked in any of the many ways that will be obvious to the imaginative reader. For example, blacksmith women do not become sexually available, nor are mourning women assigned to their waterhole. Instead, the anti-motivation that I suggested we bear in mind in chapter 3 is brought into play.[60] Those close to the dead can have no part of the utensils made by the smiths. To say that a smith cannot handle the dead because he is unclean seems an odd mode of thought in a culture that cures like with like in the area of *zaase* pollutions. This is the old problem of Mauss (1972: 97). But both are linked by a common concern with motivation through the structured perception of similarities.

In the structuring of relations between blacksmith and Dowayo rainchief, the circumciser holds a curiously ambiguous position that is perhaps relevant here. I have mentioned that amongst the other tribes of the area it is normally the blacksmith who holds responsibility for both circumcision and the disposal of the dead — including the removal of their heads. We can imagine quite easily how such a system would work. The blacksmith would be associated with heat, fire, dirt, death, while the rainchief would be associated with cool, water, cleansing and fertility — a neat binary opposition. Unfortunately no information is available on waterjars among these peoples, who makes them and how — if at all — they are used ritually. For, in the Dowayo system, the blacksmiths' potter wives, with their associations of water and birth, are a potential severe complication, while the rainchief has a temporal modality that makes him responsible for the hot, dry season and the first use of fire in the fields. The result is that the potters end up with the 'drying' end of wetness — childbirth — while the rainchiefs are allocated the 'wetting' end of dryness i.e. circumcision (at which they are present and pass on the secrets of rain to their heir) (see fig. 51). In all this, the circumciser acts as a kind of dummy for the blacksmith. He may have contact with the rainchief while — at any age — he may eat raw sesame. The problems posed by these internal complications reach their peak in the manufacturing of the rainpots which — of course — have to be made by a female blacksmith. They can only be made by a very old woman, in the dry season, at night, in the 'dead men's shelter'. They are then brought to the rainchief *not* by the sorcerer who can handle the dead but by the circumciser.

If we accept the circumciser as a surrogate blacksmith owing to internal complications of the system and the importance of the wet/dry opposition, we may begin a new approach to the question of the smoked-meat meal, beginning with the seasons of the year.

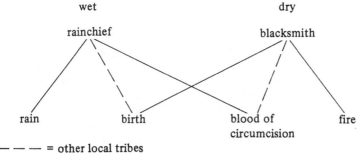

— — — = other local tribes

Figure 51

8 The seasons of the year and the joker in the pack: relations of nesting and quotation

The first division in time is into 'male' and 'female' years. Alternate years are male and female respectively. Circumcision can only happen in a male year. The main internal division of the year is into wet and dry seasons, with intermediate periods between them (fig. 52).

A skull-festival can only be held during the wet season as can the *rohtumyo* jar-ceremony. The 'sticking of the bow' occurs only in the dry season. The circumcision rites begin in the rainy season and continue until the beginning of the dry season (fig. 52). There is another event reserved for the dry season, the *waalgbaro* 'doorstep of the skull-house', when the environs of this hut are cleaned and the structure reroofed. This is often amalgamated with the *donyo* agricultural rites and, in some areas, is inseparable from them. The village may also be swept, cleaned and 'repaired' at this time.

It is clear from fig. 52 that the opposition wet/dry orders the ritual cycle. After the information presented in figs. 40 and 41 and the constant identification of pots and heads, it will come as no surprise to learn that the end of the rains, the drying of the rainstones, the firing of the mountain called 'Boy's Head', the baking of the pots, the shaving of the *donyo* organisers' heads, the removal of growth from the skull-house and the roasting of the first millet 'heads' all occur at the same time.

It seems, however, that the association of the skulls and rainfall is only half the story. The rainchief sends, it is true, the wet season but he also begins the dry season. The skulls, too, have their temporal modality being copiously anointed in the wet-season skull-festivals and only sparingly (if at all) at the start of the dry weather.[61]

There is a certain appropriateness in the return of the circumcised boys with the harvest and we have looked at this in connection with the 'beating to death of the old Fulani woman', but this has to be seen in more general terms of wet and dry.

Uncircumcised boys are in a middle position. They are male but contain elements of femininity. The Dowayos express this by saying – in accordance with their use of smell as the major mechanistic device – that boys smell 'bad', 'like women'. This is attributed to the wetness of their penes under the foreskin. In this sense then, the passage from boy to full man involves moving from wet to dry.

Girls move the other way. From an undifferentiated position, they move towards wetness at the onset of menstruation. They become vessels for conserving wetness and the waterholes are their concern.

At circumcision, the boys follow a long route from undifferentiated wetness. It will be recalled that the boy is cut in a riverside grove, kneels in the running water for several days and expects to be heavily rained upon. During this time, he must avoid all static water-holes, but bathes frequently in running water. As the weather dries out, he removes himself gradually from the river, going towards the mountains. The point where he

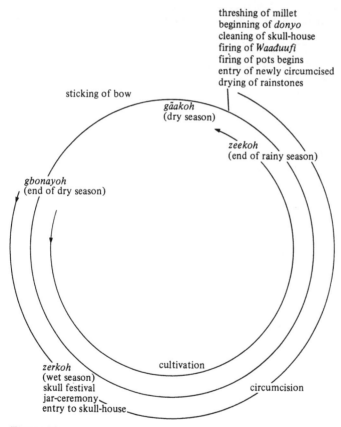

Figure 52

is allowed to wander in the bush is called *memlootemyo* 'the stirring up of the water'.[62] When he finally returns to the village, he is bathed in the river for one more time, by his 'husband' who waves burning grass over his head. It will be recalled that one part of the rite involves igniting the hut over the boys' heads while they flee to the mountains. The return occurs at the turning point from wet to dry in the calendar, at the moment when the mountain, 'Boy's Head', is fired. The boys have moved decisively from wet to relatively dry, moreover their wetness is the wetness of rainfall and moving water not of static water. This fits in well with the swift period-icity of male orgasm as opposed to the gentler rhythms of the female cycle and confirms the formulation of fig. 37. This drying is associated quite explicitly with the baking of pots and the consequent hardness of their skulls. Very young children are buried without any ceremony until 'their heads are hard'. The soft spot on a boy's head is held to harden after cir-cumcision so that it is generally believed that men have tougher heads than women.

The same distinction between the inherent wetness of women and the relative dryness of men is maintained in the contrast between the 'sticking of the bow' ceremony and the women's jar-ceremony. The former is held in the dry season, involving flowing water and the use of firebrands. The latter must be held in the rainy season and involves copious anointings inside and out, the jar being a receptacle for wetness. In the wet season, the bow of a 'true hunter' is attached to the *naamyaagyo* wild animal shrine. Only in the dry season is it used. At the wet-season skull-festival, having undergone 'circumcision', it is made into the bow bundle and placed on the *wagle*. It thus enters into the *wagle*/skull-house cycle of fig. 53 (cf. fig. 26, p. 36) and the association between head-removal and rain-fall. It is to be noted that a fire is kept burning by the head of the deceased circumcised man, at his burial, and his head comes to rest inside a hut whereas a woman's head remains exposed to the elements.

This is the point at which we must also consider the matter of agama lizards and 'firecloths'. Agama lizards are dark blue but have heads of a brilliant flame orange colour. Dowayos declare, and apparently zoology confirms it, that they emerge in the morning a rather dull dark colour but

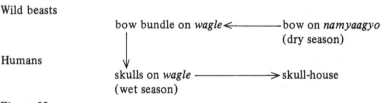

Figure 53

assume their flame-coloured head pigmentation as the sun strikes them. (Dowayos do not accept that the dull-brown females belong to the same species.) The lizards are held to be very dangerous to children and lead to 'hot heads', i.e. fevers. Circumcision candidates, however, and sometimes rich dead men wear 'firecloths' (fig. 54) around their heads. These are decorated with depictions of agama lizards. Dowayos greatly treasure these cloths and declare them − apparently erroneously − to be Fulani battle standards taken at a great massacre of their enemies. It is to be noted that it is the circumciser alone who has the remedies for the 'hot heads' provoked by contact with these beasts. The 'hot heads' recall the 'hot hands' of the blacksmith and hunter, the association of the animals with human killing, heat and circumcision in a typical 'associational cluster' as in the 'old Fulani woman' cluster (above). The agama has other functions as regards circumcision and death, often of the most redundant sort. For example, at their first entry to the skull-house (Appendix II (k)), the boys carry knives whose handles ('heads' in the Dowayo tongue) are covered with skin from the heads of agama lizards. They put these in their mouths (heads). Each stage of their progress is thus marked by a relentless coding of their heads as 'dry'.

Figure 54

Given the significance of 'heads' in Dowayo symbolism, one might reasonably ask about the penis. Does the penis, too, have a 'head'? Unfortunately, this is a question to which I can give only an unsatisfactory answer. Some circumcisers referred to the discarded foreskin (cf. millet husks) as the 'head', others to the glans. This seems to be an area where the verbal code has simply not made up its mind about two different possibilities. Is the glans of the circumcised penis to be regarded as the 'head' or is it the foreskin? The indeterminacy is also found – ritually – in millet in the distinction between that millet seed thrown on the skull-house and the husks hung on the *wagle*.

As regards the 'wet' end of the opposition, we may care to note that removal of heads is always associated with running water. The removal of rainchiefs' heads is discouraged as it would cause rainfall. Similarly, the skulls of those who have died of dysentery are not removed on pain of a universal flux. It is considered to be a mark of good fortune if it rains at a skull-festival or a jar-ceremony. These can only occur during the wet season.

Having established the importance of the wet/dry opposition, let us now return to the smoked-meat meal and the sesame or salt sauce that we left at the end of the last chapter.

At various points I have alluded to the Dowayo rites of circumcision that I describe fully in the appendix. Hitherto, I have pointed out merely how the 'beating to death of the old Fulani woman' is used to resolve various structural cruces. But circumcision, in the idiom of the Fulani woman, is far more than that. It is an armature that structures every process of social transformation. (I use the term 'armature' here in the sense of Levi-Strauss (1970: 199) though his usage elsewhere is far from consistent.) Whereas Levi-Strauss above anyone has pushed the claims of a paradigmatic as opposed to a syntagmatic analysis of myths (1964: 206), we often find temporal ordering maintained across transformations (1970: 209). In other words, temporal order in one domain may well correlate with temporal order in another. It is the circumcision rites that structure all stages of dealing with the newly dead.

Both the drawn-out rites to lay the dead to their final rest and the processes of circumcision end up in the skull-house and care is taken to establish correspondences at all stages. Both involve a stage associated with leopards in the bush, re-entry to the village, association with yams at the *wagle*, final entry to the skull-house. The circumcision ends, like the skull-festival, with the eating of smoked meat and millet with raw sesame.[63]

It is at this point that the twin associations of the smoked-meat meal are both heavily motivated externally. The boys are fully entering into male culture after wearing only leaves and dwelling in rude shelters in the bush, partly bereft of speech. They are now decked out with all the material wealth and ornamentation of which the Dowayos are capable. But they also have just returned from the house where the dead 'live'. They have returned from the wild to full incorporation in cultural manhood and are given the most elaborate meal that Dowayos possess. But it is food that verges on the rotten through its smell and the excrement that goes into the fabrication of the salt. Shop-bought salt cannot be used to make this sauce. It is also a meat characterised by dryness at the time when the boys have completed adjustment with regard to water and are about to eat raw sesame like blacksmiths. For sesame is above all a dry plant, harvested at the height of the dry season and eaten raw only by 'dry' blacksmiths. One possible interpretation of the smoked-meat meal would then be to derive other uses, e.g. that for dogs (note 63), from this strongly motivated case, using some secondary process.

The occurrence of cooked, not raw, sesame as the sauce of the meat might seem to pose a problem in that this is the form of sesame for those of unmarked ritual status. The Dowayos might have chosen this to mark the return to normality that follows the meal, but its simultaneous accompaniment by smoked meat and raw sesame strikes a distinctly jarring note. One might suggest that the rules of Dowayo cuisine permit raw sesame as a dressing stuck to millet but demand that meat be presented in a sauce which is inevitably cooked. We thus have interference between two cultural sets. We shall see shortly that this motivation of the smoked-meat meal can be replaced by one of greater generality.

It is true that when the relatives of the dead eat smoked meat and cooked sesame at each stage on the route to the skull-house, we can perceive a general direct external motivation and appropriateness, but this should not lead us to ignore the decidedly derivative look of most rites when compared to circumcision. Thus, the behaviour of the widows (Appendix I (j), (k)), after the skulls have been placed in the skull-house, replicates that of the boys for the entry to the skull-house. Even the name is retained – *dombewo hi zuul sãakoh* 'the circumcised push their heads in'. Similarly, the song that widows sing after eating ('hitherto we have all slept together, now I shall fart in my hut and you in yours') requires much less in the way of supplementary explanation if we can refer it back to the 'official version' of circumcision and joking between brothers of circumcision, than if we take it to allude directly to the women. Sometimes, too, both men and women 'swear on their knives' at this point. For men this is perfectly reasonable in that it is one of the privileges normally accorded to the circumcised. But for a woman to do it is quite extraordinary. This is not to deny that the same theme of liminality and inversion when dealing with the dead can be invoked, but, whereas clowns, brothers of circumcision and *duuse* are liminal in themselves, there is no question of their adopting a whole repertoire of dress and action from others. Let us, purely provisionally, derive the 'smoked-meat meal' from the circumcision rite and consider the other relationships we might expect to find when one rite is modelled on another (fig. 55). We shall return to the problem shortly.

We might expect to find wholesale 'quoting' as in the cases just described. This, were it completely carried through, would lead to a ritual system where all the anthropologist had to do was establish the appropriateness of a quotation. Rituals would now have assumed the function of proverbs, imposing the same structure on different matter.

We might expect to find shifts in motivation. Thus, in the case of 'the circumcised push their heads in' the yams might occupy a quite different place. We have discussed this yam in some detail (above). I opposed it to millet and connected it to hunting and death. But, just as the circumcised have to come to terms with this as they emerge from the state of boyhood, so women have to reach a new relationship with it after the period of widowhood. Both widows and boys are forbidden to consume this yam or come into contact with it until they have undergone this special meal. It is after this rite that women become available for marriage to a dead man's brother or son. If circumcision is being carried out in a village celebrating the *donyo*, the eating of the first fruit of this yam will be postponed until the entry of the circumcised to the village. Thus, internal release of the fruits of the fields (male) and the dryness of the circumcised boys are collapsed together with the release of widows for marriage to outsiders.[64] The women are marked for dryness by rubbing dried fish on their vaginas (Appendix I (d)) and closure by eating the sauce containing the floor-sealing plant *bohle* (fig. 56).

There seem, too, to be points of mutual adjustment. Thus, a boy terms the man who decorates him before circumcision 'husband'. Only later does he become 'father'. The man is often a SiHu. The object of circumcision is viewed as removing femininity from the boy and the appellation might be a reflex of this. Alternatively, it might derive from the figure of the old Fulani woman, the boy being bracketed with her. The widows, however,

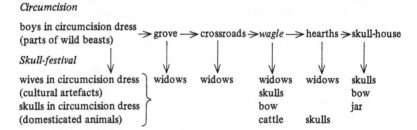

Figure 55 Distribution of roles

who adopt the dress and behaviour of these boys, really are dealing with husbands, albeit dead ones, while (Appendix I (c)) skull-festivals witness live husbands who return girls born in the village and dress them up as Fulani men.

Similarly, the dances performed, one on top of the other's shoulders, at a rich man's funeral (Appendix V (g), (k), (p)) are accompanied by the battle-song, played when a man or leopard is killed and when the skulls of the dead are carried on the shoulders of the *duuse* at the skull-ceremony (Appendix I (g)). Since a rich man is responsible for the circumcision of others and for organising the skull-festival to which poor men attach themselves, his role in these rites is prefigured at his funeral.

A ritual system that deals in self-reference and quoting must face up to problems of variation. Let us take as example the circumcision candidate. At his first decoration, apart from Fulani dress, he wears *sole* grass, horns of 'cattle-like' wild beasts, goat- and sheep-skins, leopard-skin, horsetails and firecloth.[65] This compares with other decorated forms as in fig. 57.

The dress of the circumcision candidate is identical to that of the dead except that in the former the horns of 'cattle-like' wild beasts and leopard-skin replace cattle-skin. In other words, the circumcision candidate is aligned with the wild end of the domesticated category while the cadaver is marked as 'domesticated'. By the time we deal with the skull-festival adornments of the deceased, millet-sticks and cockerel feathers have been added and the bundle is flanked by the dancing cattle-skins and yam-bow group, all of which are mobile as the candidate was before. It will be recalled that all are placed on the *wagle*, as part of the 'domestication of death'. At the same time, the *dōre* witnesses a passage in the opposite direction in the presence of the death-drum, an instrument in the form of a mortar for removing the 'heads' of millet and containing the stone 'leopard's neckbone'.

All the attributes of a man's life are thus assembled from all domains of experience, and passed through the *wagle* as the gateway to the area of undifferentiation.

The decorated jar (Appendix IV (d)) differs from the decorated circum-

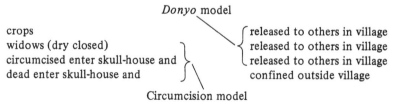

Figure 56

cision candidate in the absence of any 'wild' element. The broad hoes used are sometimes called 'women's horns' and were apparently the traditional means of payment to the rainchief in times of drought. The 'hands of the rain', special ritual irons, are derived morphologically from throwing irons and allegedly were once used by the rainchief to cause lightning (an attribute of 'female' rain). Beads and *helle* grass also occur at this point.

Helle, apart from being the name of a species of grass, is also the word for 'broom' (a 'broom' consists of a bunch of this grass). At the end of the jar-ceremony, women dance with brooms in their hands. It might at first seem odd that women should be heavily marked with cultural artefacts, while men move between wild and domesticated beasts. We should note,

Dead male	Circumcision	Entry to skull-house
Blue robe[66]	Blue robe	Burial cloth
white robe	white robe	red knives
feathers	feathers	horsetails
bosohse bark	*bosohse* bark	goat-skin/sheep-skin
sole grass	*sole* grass	beads
burial cloth	burial cloth	bracelets
red hat	red hat	
firecloth	firecloth	
goat-skin/sheep-skin	horsetails	
cattleskins	goat-skin/sheep-skin	
	leopardskin	

Male skulls	*Rohtumyo* jar	Wives at skull-festival
Blue robe	Blue robe	(Appendix I (c))
white robe	white robe	
feathers	*belnaane* 'rain irons'	Blue robe
bosohse bark	*bosohse* bark	white robe
burial cloth	*sole* grass	red hat
red hat	burial cloth	Fulani weapons
firecloth	red hat	Fulani calabashes
horsetails	firecloth	Fulani tassles
goat-skin/sheep-skin	horsetails	wrist-watches
	goat-skin/sheep-skin	sunglasses
	beads	money
	bracelets	
	helle grass	
	hoe blades	

Figure 57

however, that for the Dowayos these are not just cultural artefacts, but artefacts of foreign origin. They were all made long ago by foreign smiths, some Fulani, some Dupa. The songs sung during the festival are in Pape or Tchamba, as well as Dowayo. The link between foreignness, culture and women lies, I suggest, in the beating to death of the old Fulani woman. The motivation of these variations on the dress of the circumcision candidate lies itself in the role of foreign women as mediators of culture.

The presence of the beads and bracelets must be related to other cultural rules about decoration. After the death of a man, his wives should eschew all body decoration until the celebration of the skull-festival. Even ochre and oil should not be rubbed on the body until the head of the corpse has been similarly treated. For the death of a wife, similar rules obtain but bracelets and rings may be worn by the husband after the decoration of the water-jar. (It will be recalled that the name of the ceremony *rohtumyo* means 'decoration'; see fig. 57.) This may serve as confirmatory evidence that the jar-ceremony serves the same function for women as the skull-festival for men. We note, to generalise a 'theme', that self-decoration is only possible once the dead have been decorated, purely social dancing only allowed once they have 'danced' too.

This theme holds quite generally down to quite small particulars. Thus, at the 'sticking of the bow', the widow wears a piece of pot on her head while several similar pieces are attached to the ends and middle of her deceased husband's bow. It is to be remembered that this bow is normally kept on the *namyaagyo* shrine of a hunter, with the heads and necks of killed game. At the end of the festival it is attached at the back of the skull-house. The association with heads is continued at the skull-festival. The organiser's bow is brought out with the skulls and decorated as they are. At the end, it passes into the skull-house.

The objects attached to it at the 'sticking of the bow' are interesting. Broken pot associates it firmly with the widow's head. The leaves involved are used for making the head-pads when carrying pots and other burdens. The stone *ɗaatsumoh* 'ants' death-drum' is attached to the area called globally 'navel'. Thus, the bow is given both 'heads' and a 'belly' and is 'circumcised'. The belly is assigned to the ants — the eaters of wood in Africa — as the bellies of cattle are cooked and thrown over the death drum of men — the eaters of cattle. So the bow enters into the head/skull/pot/stone cycle. The head of the woman is associated with the bow of her husband, placed outside the village, at the moment she becomes available to marriage outside the group. Once more, 'sticking of bow', jar-ceremony and skull-festival show a common armature (fig. 58). But there is a further point here. I have dwelt at some length on the systematic importance of the wet/dry opposition. If we consider the presence of the rain-irons as decoration on the water-jar, it becomes clear what this decoration would most closely resemble, if such a thing occurred. It is, in fact, a close analogue of an absent term — the rainmaker's skull-ceremony. The fact that the jar-ceremony replaces the skull-ceremony as the device moving women from the differentiated state of individuals to that of undifferentiated spirit lends further weight to this equation. I have stated that there is a coalescence in rainmaker villages between various levels of the system that relates humans, plants and rainfall with a water-jar replacing the human skull (figs. 40 and 41).

Why should the idiom of the rainmaker be used at this particular point? I would suggest that this is again connected with the distinction between rainfall and still water. This, after all, is the point at which a woman ceases to be a receptacle of spirit and still water. She now becomes capable of fertilising women herself — as spirit — a task for which the association with rainfall becomes appropriate. The use of the water-jar at this point thus operates to resolve a structural crux, just as the use of the *Tarniisnohg-barklele* myth handles the problem raised by the threshing of a 'true cultivator's' millet.

The use of zero elements that are realised at subsequent levels of analysis only, need not concern us unduly. It is, like all powerful formal devices, subject to abuse but justifiable by and answerable to the criterion of overall simplification that we invoke more generally in symbolic analysis. As a linguistic device it is of sound pedigree and quite standard at all levels.

There is yet another element to be considered in this rite that relates it to more general concepts of pollution through inappropriate relations with cultural objects.

I have already referred to the category *zaase* ('pollution') when we were considering representational symbolism in pots. Excessive contact with blacksmiths causes disease. The knife of circumcision also causes a form of *zaase*, while rainchiefs are responsible for a *zaase* in the form of the worms that invade a man's body during the rains. Contact with certain plants causes *zaase*. (There is a plant, for example, *buuyo*, that produces swollen seed pods. Children are warned never to play with these on pain of suffering from a distended belly like the pod.) The sorcerer's *zaase* comes from contact with the belongings of the dead or stolen property.[67] Inevitably, in Dowayoland, some of these dangerous objects get drawn into the ambit of the skull/stone/pot group. There exist named magic stones, owned by

'Sticking of bow' releases woman to outsiders again for marriage
Jar-ceremony releases woman to outsiders again for skull-festival
Skull-festival releases woman to insiders again for marriage

Figure 58

particular families, that cause stillbirth, toothache, dysentery and other ills (fig. 59). A person afflicted by such a stone must seek out the owner and give money or millet which is offered to the stone. The owner will then either rub the stone on the afflicted part to cure it; or a herbal remedy, kept apart in a pot, will be used.[68]

There is a class of *zaase* coming from everyday household objects, such as hoes, granaries, hearths. These afflict children in particular. The children, instead of being fattened by the produce of these objects, become thin and sickly. The cure consists of decorating the child with beads, ochre, iron bracelets and all the finery worn by widows and boys when they return from skull-festival and skull-house respectively. Here also use is made of the smoked-meat meal, which I have suggested to be particularly well motivated for the visit to the skull-house after circumcision and possibly derived from here by secondary process. The child is simply placed in the granary (any section) or crouches with the hearth between his legs and is rubbed with the hoes. The left foot of a chicken is cut and blood rubbed on the offending object and the child's head. The hair is cut in a star shape.

Dowayos explain that this is done 'so that his forehead will be rough'

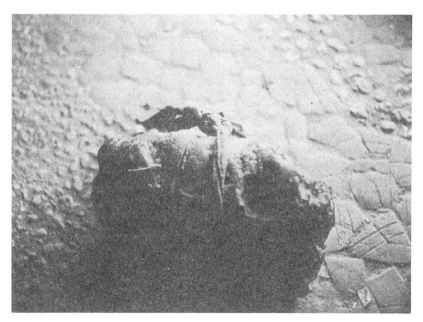

Figure 59

(*An tīil oh hāa*). Further questioning evokes the information 'rough – like a dog's'. The point is that dogs are considered lucky beasts in that wherever they go they find food.[69] A similar practice is adopted at the festivals. Spectators' foreheads are daubed with either red ochre or blood which has been smeared on skulls, *looreyo* jars, water-jars and the head of the clown and relatives of participants.[70] The festivals have the explicit aim of adjusting relationships between all these elements.

It thus seems likely that we should best regard the smoked-meat meal as a manifestation of the more general class of *zaase* rich food, while the decoration of the water-jar would represent a collapsing together of the dress of a circumcision candidate (including adaptations for 'rainchief') and the ornamentation involved in the resolution of pollution from cultural objects.

We are now in a position to suggest some of these nestings and mergings in more general terms. Circumcision itself would divide – in standard anthropological manner – into separation (liminality) and integration. Separation is expressed in terms of 'the beating to death of the old Fulani woman' plus adaptations. Integration is expressed in terms of *donyo* (minimal meals, use of *wagle*, 'scorpions' food, avoidance of instruments of culture), and *zaase* (richly elaborated food, body decoration, star-haircut, touching of heads, formation of new relations with cultural objects).

The skull-festival, on the other hand, is modelled on the rites of circumcision, so that we have a nesting of the form:

I Skull-festival (circumcision ('beating to death of . . . etc.' plus (*donyo* plus *zaase*)))

i.e. the skull-festival is expressed in terms of circumcision which in turn is expressed in terms of the 'beating to death of the old Fulani woman' plus *donyo* together with *zaase*.

Whereas events at the skull-ceremony clearly derive their structure from circumcision, relations between this festival and *donyo* or *zaase* show no clear directionality. The present formulation is adopted merely on grounds of simplicity of the overall description.

Examination of the jar-ceremony suggests the analysis:

II Rainchief's skull-festival (circumcision ('beating to death . . . etc.' plus *zaase*))

i.e. there is no trace of *donyo* elements.

This confirms our view of 'woman as a cultural object' and suggests the revision of I to allow for this variation, giving III:

III Skull-festival (circumcision ('beating to death . . . ' plus
$\left\{ \begin{array}{l} \textit{zaase})) \\ \textit{donyo} \text{ plus } \textit{zaase})) \end{array} \right\}$

Analysis III also handles the main features of the 'sticking of the bow'
ceremony quite adequately. But, if we regard elements such as the entry to
the skull-house and the decoration of the jar as manifestations of *zaase*,
there is an important difference where the bow is concerned. There is no
question of decoration here in beads, bracelets, etc. The only element of
zaase in the widow's dress is the assumption of the star-shaped haircut.
There is another conflicting principle in operation here — the interdiction
on the decoration of the spouse until the dead have been ornamented. In
the case of the jar, which plays the same structural role as the skull-
ceremony in the change from differentiated to non-differentiated, to
decorate the pot is to decorate the woman. In the case of a man's bow,
this does not hold. His skull has yet to be ornamented at the skull-festival.
A precise formal system to trace such 'interferences' between the rules of
cultural symbolism does not as yet exist and, indeed, may prove imposss-
ible. The hope of some such mapping device raises the possibility, however, of a formal procedure for deciding when a jar 'represents' a woman's
skull, or whatever, while a man's bow does not; i.e. the possibility of ultimately expressing external motivation in terms of the combination and
interaction of ordered internal rules. We have also seen that several routes
may be followed to motivate a single element. Thus, in dealing with the
smoked-meat meal with sesame or salt sauce, we looked at the possibility
of external motivation (associations with death, rottenness and dryness),
internal classifications (involving the blacksmith) and the process by which
it could be derived analogically from the position of the boys at the circumcision ritual. It was finally suggested that it should be referred to the
more comprehensive category of *zaase* pollution in the interests of the
greater general simplicity of the description thus arrived at. The alternative
motivations still remain but are redundant and *relatively* arbitrary in their
ad hoc quality. This is not to say that the extension of the analysis into
other areas might not reverse this position, since the point at which we
decide to stop is a matter of judgment.

Likewise, the fact that the circumcision candidate is a 'wife' to his
sponsor was referred both to an interplay between those assigned this role
at the rites of circumcision and the skull-festival and to the explicit
femininity of the boy in his uncut condition. It will be noted that motivation via 'the beating to death of the old Fulani woman' used as an idiom
of circumcision and separation subsumes both.

It is a matter of some interest that the 'adaptations' looked at when a
ritual from one area is 'quoted' in another are the most *ad hoc* part of the

description, the point where the yield is lowest for the understanding of the cultural system. The higher-level elements *zaase, donyo* etc. reduce to extremely general types of symbolic mechanisms concerned with problems of social classification. When we are dealing with ceremonies of this well-defined sort, models involving nesting, quotation and concatenation are most useful. But the formulations offered (I–III) can have only a schematic ordering value. They are derived loosely from linguistic models and this is both their strength and their weakness. Their strength lies in their ability to formalise relations. Their weakness lies in the fact, attested throughout this work, that symbolism is *not* language. The latter works almost entirely with arbitrary, structured matter, hence its suitability to all forms of transformational operations that leave its original structure unimpaired and recoverable. Symbolism is arbitrary always to a limited degree and seeks to move from the arbitrary to the motivated, harnessing all forms of knowledge and classification to this end. Immediate external motivation of the crassest form is always available to short-circuit the elaborate classifications and operations that have constituted its primary matter. Thus, in fig. 60, which attempts to summarise the place of Dowayo water-jars in the cultural system, the interpretation of the water-jar as a 'womb', were it only slightly strengthened by some minor embellishments, would risk the whole delicate fabric of the 'skull' complex and make it irretrievable to analysis.

Such very simple formal structures as are used here, let it again be said, are far from novel in linguistic practice. The fact that they are so pervasive in Dowayo symbolism entails nothing for other systems of other peoples. The truly comparative study of symbolic systems is still in its infancy.

Collapsing and nesting at a deep level involves no special pleading, therefore. At the level of sheer performance such phenomena can be readily observed in Dowayo life. The exigencies of convenience figure largely in what appears 'on the ground'. Thus, men in mourning will appear in the appropriate leaves at a 'sticking of the bow' ceremony when, in theory, they should be naked. Dowayos will frequently perform a skull-ceremony and an 'entry to the skull-house' (Appendix II (k)) at the same time in order to take advantage of the presence of beer and the necessary kinsmen. There is a considerable shortage of proper ritual paraphernalia. Even the most central elements, e.g. a leopard skin at circumcision, may be omitted if unavailable. Everyone knows how it should be done and one does the best one can in any given circumstances.[71]

One also elaborates as best one can. One man caused quite a stir at a skull-festival when he returned his wife to her native village dressed as a male Fulani but added the element of thousand-franc notes and old lottery tickets pinned to her head. Another innovated by dressing in the Fulani outfit to climb on the hut roof of his brother of circumcision at the end of

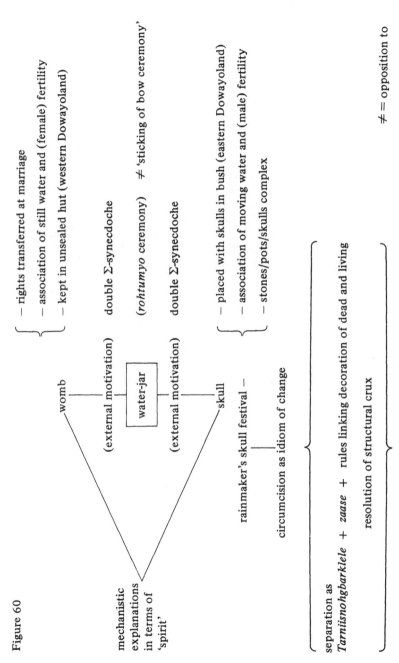

Figure 60

– rights transferred at marriage
– association of still water and (female) fertility
– kept in unsealed hut (western Dowayoland)

womb

(external motivation)

water-jar

(external motivation)

skull

double Σ-synecdoche

(*rohtumyo* ceremony) ≠ 'sticking of bow ceremony'

double Σ-synecdoche

– placed with skulls in bush (eastern Dowayoland)
– association of moving water and (male) fertility
– stones/pots/skulls complex

mechanistic
explanations
in terms of
'spirit'

rainmaker's skull festival –

circumcision as idiom of change

separation as
Tarniisnohgbarklele + *zaase* + rules linking decoration of dead and living

resolution of structural crux

≠ = opposition to

the skull-festival. This caused much discussion, the old men regarding it as indulgent ostentation, the young men tending to admire it.

The formal, componential analyses of Dowayo festivals call to mind, however, not simply linguistic models but also those of musical form. After *The Raw and the Cooked* (Levi-Strauss 1970), it cannot be claimed that this is a particularly novel insight, but simply an expression of the predominance of internal over external motivation and the cohesion of the festivals as a whole. They have in common the insistent use of a limited set of elements that are varied and recombined and whose reference thereby is to each other rather than to the outside world. In this sense, Dowayo culture has a determinedly involuted and closed aspect. It is, in fact, neither the specifically musical nor the markedly linguistic nature of such models that makes them suitable for use in symbolic analysis. It is rather their ability to formalise basic logical relationships.

It is only in those areas where external motivation is relatively strong that we can employ tropic models borrowed from poetics and speak of metaphor, synecdoche and relevance restrictions. Elsewhere in the system, internal motivation takes over and we see the link between poetic experience and symbolicity to lie in those processes by which the arbitrary is reduced to the motivated.

In this culture, the rite of circumcision itself seems to play something of the role of a joker. It is made to figure in any game the culture may be playing whether this be the removal of the heads of the millet, the return of a dead woman to her village, the entry of a dead man into the skull/stone opposition or the adjustment of a boy's relations with water or femininity. The result is a patchwork quilt of material that may be more or less appropriate to its context, the product of an act of *bricolage*. But it cannot be claimed, I think, that these festivals make any profound propositional statement about the nature of life, death or man's place in the cosmos.

The system described here is not a coherent statement of propositions about what anthropologists have loosely termed a 'world-view'. It is primarily an attempt to build with prefabricated units and reduce the unknown to the known.

The investigation that began with the question: 'What does the water-jar mean?' has led a long way, with many circuitous detours through sub-systems and offshoots of Dowayo culture.

I hope it at least suffices to show that questions such as this, let alone the quite different question: 'Why do Dowayos do this?', cannot be answered in such terms and may be deemed almost irrelevant to the task of analysis. I have stressed throughout that the scope of this book is one of fairly low-level description of a particular culture. The task of true explanation remains.

The present study has sought to explore some of the mechanisms that structure Dowayo culture, especially the relationship between analyses which depend on internal motivation and those which employ external relations. A question for comparative ethnography will be how far a different balance between the two constitutes an important difference in 'cultural style', as opposed to a mere bias of either the ethnographer or the conscious models of his subjects. We cannot know either, at this stage, what the implications may be of such a slanting of the culture towards one or the other possibility. Does it affect a culture's ability to resist or adapt to change?

A major problem of current studies remains the inadequacy of present forms of transcription. In the investigation of symbolic structures we are working in an area at the outer limits of language. Hence the structuralist use of diagrams, matrices etc. Concern with transcription is rather more than the desire to be as precise in our formulations as possible, though this remains a laudable aim. In the linguistic sciences, it has been found that improved forms of transcription make possible the evaluation of competing explanations according to measures of general simplicity. In anthropology, as I hope to have demonstrated in the evolution of the various maps describing the Dowayo symbolic space, they enter into our deliberations as a form of discovery procedure, through our presupposition that symbolic forms will tend towards regularity of structure. It is to be hoped that future research will lead to advances in this area and so make possible analyses that – at the moment – would be impossible to perform.

The analyses presented here have centred on ceremonial activity, though it has proved unnecessary to restrict ourselves to this domain. In many ways this focus is unfortunate since it encourages us to believe that there exists a form of activity called 'ritual' separated from other forms of behaviour. In the depiction of the use made of circumcision to structure other kinds of process, such as threshing or skull-removal, we have been able to speak of simple unidirectional metaphor. In other areas, it is far less self-evident that we should think in such terms. The equation of the changes in human state with the potting process suggests far more a mutual reciprocal influence than the structuring of 'ritual' by technology. This begins to look like a Western ethnocentric view. An argument could be made, for example, that the notorious lack of technical proficiency of Dowayo potters and their dogged refusal to adopt a semi-kiln firing technique require an explanation that involves symbolic process. Technological change in this area would gravely disrupt the parallel between the firing of pots and the heaping up and 'firing' of the circumcision candidates (Appendix II (g)), Dowayo rules about inside and outside and the parallel between the threshing floor and the potters' fire. We seem here to have not so much metaphor as disparate activities that we would variously classify as 'ritual' or 'technology' that are commonly structured at some deeper level, i.e. metonymic process. The value of this distinction and its relevance for the dissection of the catch-all anthropological notion of metaphor remain to be established.

While the peoples of North Cameroon constitute a fascinating and rich ethnographic kaleidoscope, constantly rearranging similar institutions into different patterns, it is hoped that the issues raised here may be relevant to workers in totally unrelated areas. It is something of an act of faith that, while the material it calls into play may vary, symbolic process is part of the universal equipment of mankind and so may be studied comparatively. Were this not so, it is hard to see how cross-cultural comprehension would even be possible.

Appendix: The festivals

I Skull-festival: *zuuldukyo* ('throwing on the skulls')

(a) A Dowayo's skull-festival can be celebrated at any time after his or her death and will be organised by patrilineal kinsmen. Often this is the result of a member of the family being plagued by dreams of the dead person which leads to an expectation that he will be afflicted with disease by the spirit of the deceased unless steps are taken. The festival requires much in goats, millet and cattle and a man will expect to gain much prestige from a successful skull-festival. Normally, all the skulls of recently dead in the same skull-house, and possibly associated blacksmiths will be involved. The financial arrangements are simplest when all herd communally, otherwise payments will have to be made. A man begins by inviting kin and affines to a beer party where the topic is raised. If this passes off well, a second party is organised. If this too passes without incident, the omens are taken.

A sheep is led to the dead men's shelter and stretched on its back. The skin is cut off the back legs and rest of the body except for the forepaws and head. If it suffers this without excessive complaint, the time is held to be appropriate. The beast is killed and the excrement flung on the skulls. A date is fixed in the rainy season. Not only kinsmen attend a skull-festival. Friends and strangers flock in equal numbers to the scene, often travelling overnight on foot. It is not unusual to find some six hundred to a thousand Dowayos present at one time. Activities are spread over a number of days. Preparations include the grinding of millet for beer and the renewing of all gateways, especially the *wagle*, the gate on which the skulls of the dead cattle are displayed. A new *dōre* is also set up. These are rubbed with red ochre. Affines bring cattle, skins, burial cloth and millet. Skins and burial cloth are placed on the *wagle*.

(b) The clowns collect the skulls, from the rear of the skull-house in the case of men, from the rear of a hut in the village in the case of women. This involves only the heads of those for whom the festival has not thus far been organised. A skull undergoes the skull-festival only once. After this it is assigned to the interior of the skull-house in the case of men. Women's skulls are placed under a tree in the bush or buried in a communal pit. The skulls are aligned on *gbohgle* grass mats in a cleared space outside the village and divided into two groups, male and female. Blacksmiths' skulls will be kept apart. The uncircumcised are placed with the women.

Goats and sheep are slaughtered and the contents of their stomachs and intestines are thrown, with the left hand, over the skulls by the organisers of the festival. The clowns too will throw and make every attempt to splash bystanders who are in their best clothes and greatly disgusted by this fetid matter. With the large numbers of people present and the humidity of the rainy season, the heat and stench are considerable. The blood of chickens will also be splashed on the skulls.

(c) During this time, affines have been coming to the village, bringing gifts. The husbands of women from the village return with them and ornament them. The women are dressed up as male Fulani warriors, carrying spears and knives. Canopies and red umbrellas will be held over them. Money may be pinned to their heads 'to show the wealth of the husband'. They dance to the tom-toms and *tiiryo* flutes which 'speak' by imitating the tones of the language. The flutes tell them to excel in dancing and not be intimidated by their neighbours. Much use is made of decorative trade goods. Many of the women wear sunglasses and watches, Fulani ornaments or the produce of Nigerian factories. They will dance for several hours outside the village before the admiring gaze of their husbands.

(d) In another part of the village, the widows have also been preparing. For the three days before the festival, they have been wearing *gbungtyo* leaves and *silkoh* grass and preparing beer. They visit their *duuse*s to collect millet. The day before the main festival (b) they leave the village in the evening, while the beer is fermenting, and spend the night together in a rough leaf shelter outside the village. At dawn, one of the women sets fire to the hut and they all flee, naked and crying out to the mountains, abandoning the leaves and calabashes they have been using. They collect the *sēkoh* leaves they will wear later and go to the place of circumcision naked. There they rub a dried fish on their anuses and vaginas (*daase*) and put on a small quantity of *diiblyoh* leaves and bark and go to the crossroads. Here, they are fed by the dead man's sister and the clown. The meal consists of smoked meat and salt brought in red pots and millet rolled in sesame in baskets. It also contains *bohle* a sticky liana used to seal floors that is otherwise forbidden to widows. They spit out the food three times and swallow the fourth time. They return to the village to welcome the skulls of their husbands.

(e) The men have been occupied in making the bow bundle. The bow of the dead man for whom the festival has been organised is brought from the skull-house to one side of the village. It is wrapped in burial cloth together with the yam called *taabmaatoh* that grows around the dead men's shelter. Two sticks of millet adorned with red and white feathers (*lulyo* and cockerel feathers) are attached to it and the men dance from village to bush with the bundle, waving weapons and singing the *yaako* circumcision song, led by the organiser who wears a hat of porcupine quills. The sorcerer rings his bell and blows his flute. All women flee. The clowns are very active in their buffoonery.

(f) The 'women of the village' (i.e. those who are neither widows nor married out) gather under a *tarko* tree where they have set up a large water-jar on a hearth. The *duuse* and the dead man's SiDa remove all jewellery and dress in *tarko* leaves. They pour into the jar beer brought by the various relatives and call out the names of the dead women. Other women lick the jar to have good fortune and become pregnant. The men have set up a similar jar without hearth under a *sēkoh* tree and the names of the dead men are called out while beer is poured into it. The men's jar often differs from the women's in that it has a removable plug that is pulled out so that the beer flows all over the earth. The men rejoin the bow bundle and dance back to the village waving weapons and singing the circumcision songs (*taabnaboh*). It is carried by the clown accompanied by sorcerer and brother of circumcision of the man for whom the festival is being organised. The men are attacked by the uncircumcised and these are driven off twice. The men place the bundle on the *wagle*.

(g) All the men now go to the skulls. Women and children may not be present. The organiser and his brothers throw cattle excrement on the skulls, cutting the heads off chickens to sprinkle their blood on the skulls. The clowns fight over the chickens and steal them. The skulls are cleaned by the clowns with *tarko* leaves and placed in a basket. The women's skulls are wrapped in a white robe and dumped to one side. The men's are wrapped in a white robe, a blue robe and a red hat. Sheep-skins, horsetails and feather sticks are attached with *bosohse* grass or narrow strips of woven cotton and long stretches of burial cloth are attached. The *wangyo* flutes are blown and the bundle is threatened with knives and menaced with circumcision. The men sing the *yaako* circumcision song. It is hefted on the head of the *duuse* who sets off, bobbing and weaving, towards the village, accompanied by men singing the *gapsnaboh* (battle-song sung when a man has killed). Before it, dance men who have put on the skins of slaughtered cattle and stamp up and down with bells round their ankles. They are greeted at the gate to the village, by the organiser ringing a bell and by a single widow in *sēkoh* leaves. After many hesitations, the bundle enters the village and circles the *dōre*. It is placed on the *wagle*. The widows dance. The organiser climbs up beside and shouts: 'I have circumcised these men. If it were not for the White Man, I should have killed a man.'

The *duuse* will later undo the bundle and the skulls will be placed in the skull-house or communal grave, for men. Women's skulls are deposited to the side of the *wagle* and will later be placed under a tree in the bush or in a communal grave. Before this, they are oiled and covered with red ochre and sprinkled with animal excrement.

(h) Feasting, dancing and drinking will continue throughout the night. The organiser, however, must now leave and may not eat, drink or sleep in the village that night.

(i) The men bring up their beer-jar and rub oil and red ochre on it. The dead man's SiDa goes to the women's beer-jar. The foot of a chicken is cut and blood smeared on the jar and the foreheads of the women. The *tarko* leaves are removed and normal dress resumed. The jars will join the skulls.

(j) The widows spend the night together on *gbohgle* mats in the public circle. The next day, they are summoned by the clown beating a hoe blade and shouting: 'Your husbands have gone inside and you too shall enter.' They go to the compound of the first wife of the dead man and are fed the smoked-meat meal with sesame or salt sauce, millet and raw sesame. They visit all the compounds of all his wives ('the visiting of the hearths') and blood from a chicken's leg is rubbed on the hearth of the first wife and the head of the man's SiDa ('because she saw them naked and must not have a smooth forehead') and the heads of the women. They may or may not be decorated with beads and bracelets. Sometimes this may not happen until after they have been to the crossroads.

(k) The widows sleep in the compound of the first wife for three days. Roots of *gbungtyo* are ground and a necklace made of the fibres. The wives throw away the *sēkoh* and change into *sebore* leaves at the cross-roads. Their hair is shaven into a star shape and they are taken to the public circle where they are given cooked *zangyo* yams to eat. These have been forbidden to them up to this time and must now be eaten without touching them with their hands or cutting them with knives. The clown places the yams between their legs and they spit out the first three mouthfuls and only swallow the fourth. They are taken to the crossroads and dressed in bracelets and necklaces and covered with oil and ochre. They dance groin to groin with their husbands' brothers who are naked but for a penis sheath and sing: 'Hitherto we have all slept together. Now I shall fart in my hut and you shall fart in yours.'

(l) The day after (g) any men from this or any other village who wish to, dress themselves up in trade goods and dance before the *wagle*. They wear rings, bracelets, sunglasses and Nigerian cottons and dance admiring themselves in mirrors. In their hair is a long cockerel feather.

(m) On the same day or the next day, the roof of the dead man's hut is decorated with *yaahutu* bark and *zepto* and white chicken feathers. A brother of circumcision of the dead man climbs on the hut and ties burial cloth from one roof to another of his compound and rubs his anus on the top of the roof. He must stay until beer is given to him, then he can come down. During this, *wangbedo* flutes are played.

II Circumcision: *domse*

(a) A boy may be circumcised at any age from about eight on. Dowayos, however, do not count years and simply stress that a boy must be 'big' enough to stand the pain. The festival begins when a rich man decides that his son is old enough to be cut. He will meet together with kinsmen and friends who wish to join in and cut their sons and all will agree, or not, to take the omens. A male goat is killed and its blood is smeared in *silkoh* grass and left at the circumcision grove by the river. If, after a couple of days, the blood has not attracted ants, the time is held to be good. The participation of the Old Man of Kpan, the principal rainmaker in Dowayo-land, is also required. The final decision depends on his omens. Divination consists of sealing certain plants (*zepto, geelyo*) in a gourd (*tiikwaalo*) and placing it in a cavern in *Waaduufi*, the rainmaker's mountain. It is sealed up and, if the gourd reappears in a whirlpool at the base of the mountain, this is thought to betoken the acceptance of the spirits of the dead of circumcision.

Sometimes, festivals may be very large, with up to a hundred youths being circumcised and twenty or thirty circumcisers. In Dowayoland, alternate years are 'male' or 'female'. Circumcision can occur only in a male year.

(b) The festival normally starts just after the beginning of the rains, when the new leaves have formed, i.e. about April. (In recent years pressure has been applied to synchronise circumcision with official school holidays and the duration of the ritual has been drastically curtailed.) The boys are taken to the shelter where the bodies of newly dead men are kept. There, their heads are completely shaven and they are given penis-sheaths and the special *sonyoh* hat. They dress in *gōkoh* leaves and carry a bent stick of hardwood and roam the countryside in bands visiting relatives and dancing in the public space before the *wagle*. Salt, pimento, sesame and *zangoh* yams are now forbidden them. The relatives lavish food of all kinds upon them and they all sleep together in the public circle on *gbohgle* mats. One particular relative has to decorate the boy in the full splendour of the circumcision outfit. Often, this will be a SiHu but not obligatorily so. The boy calls his dresser 'husband', the man calls the boy 'wife'. The boy wears a blue robe over a white one, *sole* grass round his ankles, burial cloth, a red hat, horsetails, goat- and sheep-skins, a leopard-skin and the horns of the wild buffalo (*aro*). He may also wear the 'fire-cloth', putatively a battle-flag taken from the Fulanis decorated with appliquéd images of red lizards. The boy dances with a violent shaking motion much admired by his kinsmen, as if attempting to dislodge the ornaments. He also wears small bells around his feet, that are stamped at each step. He dances to the small, curved *wangɓedo* flute. The boys return to the village and sleep in the public space. The boy breaks into his father's compound and steals beer. Sometimes, there is a preliminary visit to the circumcision grove 'to view the knives'. The smallest of the boys may not know that circumcision involves cutting the penis and suffer a considerable shock. Most, however, are well aware as this is a subject of the whispered folklore of boyhood and great store is set by the bravery of the candidate. The boys are taken out at dusk and the circumcisers roam the village with bullroarers scaring the women. The boys are given various herbal remedies and made to drink large quantities of beer. At the crossroads they are stripped naked. At some point along the way, each boy is ambushed by growling circumcisers who leap out on him, hold him against a hardwood tree and cut him while singing the *yaako* circumcision song. The Dowayo form of circumcision is very severe and the penis should be peeled for its entire length. The boy should be cut several times by different circumcisers. He will be taken to the river by his 'husband' and washed while singing the *lore* song. The *sole* grass is cut off his leg. The penis is wrapped in *furkale* 'hoe-handle' grass and the boy wears *diiblyo* bark round his waist. The boy spends three days without shelter, much of this kneeling in the river, and the men sing mocking songs. It is believed that it always rains at this time.

(c) At the end of this period, the boys go to a small hill called *Nungwohmo* 'old name' where they undo the grass from their penes and call out their names. The grass is buried under a pile of stones, the boys wash in the river and take new names. They put on *gbaanyo* leaves.

(d) After the three days, a rough leaf shelter is made for the boys. They are fed by their 'husband' who brings food from the village. The boys may not touch knives or break bones. Their food must be bland and smooth. They may not see women.

(e) After some three months, the boys are covered from head to foot in a thick coat of *gbungtayo* leaves and carry a calabash marked with a red cross hung on their backs. They are given a small flute with which they can communicate with any woman they happen to meet. This imitates the tones of the language and enables the candidate to 'speak'. He will be accompanied by his 'husband' who accepts any gifts made to him. The boy may roam around the bush. When not in this outfit, they wear a small quantity of the plant *domdapto*.

(f) Before the boys may re-enter the village they must 'beat the old Fulani woman to death'. The boys gather under a *Tarekopse* tree and crouch at either side of a path. A clown assumes the role of an old woman and the 'play' is exactly as described in chapter 6.

(g) The boys return to their hut. At dawn this is fired by a 'husband' and the boys flee naked to the mountains (by now they wear the penis sheath all the time) crying out. They gather *sēkoh* with which they cover their bodies and heads and are taken towards the village.

(h) The time at which the boys may return has suffered displacement from all sorts of official pressures. Government deplores the interference with schooling, the hospital service seeks to limit the severity of the operation, Christians scorn the whole process as barbaric and go instead to the hospital. These factors have strongly curtailed the period in the bush. Old men agree that in former times the boys should not return until the end of the rains (i.e. about the time of harvest).

(i) There follow a series of three meals that show slight variation in order and content in different parts of Dowayoland. There is an element called *sengbekyo* 'visiting the hearth'. The boys are led round the different compounds by the clown and may or may not be fed there. If they are fed, then they eat smoked meat, millet with raw sesame and native salt or cooked sesame. The foot of a chicken is cut and touched against the hearth, the clown's head and each of the boys' heads in turn. They return to the crossroads and are fed millet rolled in raw sesame. The clowns put oil and ochre on their bodies and penes. The plant 'scorpion's food' is attached to the penis. The boys put on a long white skirt. Their hair is trimmed at the temples. They go to the village and dance.

(j) In some parts of Dowayoland, *Dombewo hi zuul sāakoh* (see Appendix I (k)) follows almost immediately. In other areas, it may occur a month later. The boys wear *sebore* leaves and lianas. Their hair is cut in a star shape. The yams are forbidden to circumcision candidates and must be eaten without being touched by the hands or cut. They spit out three mouthfuls and swallow the fourth. They dance with women from the village and sing: 'Hitherto we have all slept together. Now I shall fart in my hut and you shall fart in yours'. They swear on their knives.

(k) Entry to the skull-house (*waalgulikyo*). Some time after the previous stage, the newly circumcised are taken to the skull-house for the first time. Their hair is shaven to a star-shape or in alternate stripes (see chapter 3). They dress in necklaces and bracelets, cowrie shells, goat- and sheep-skins. They are covered in oil and red ochre. They carry bows and bucklers, quivers and knives. In their mouths are small knives. Knives are tied the length of each leg.

The boys, accompanied by sorcerer and clown and any circumcised male relative who wishes to be there, go to the skull-house and drink beer from long calabashes ('male calabashes'). The men line up outside the skull-house and each has a switch of tamarind branch in his hand (*zamse*). The first youth enters the hut and the men cry out three times asking who he is. He shouts out his (new) name. The boy runs in and out four times and is beaten by all. All the boys do likewise. The men sing the battle song and all return to the village. As the boys enter the women beat them. The boys present beer to the men who were their 'husbands', and who are henceforth called 'father'.

(l) The next day, or later the same day, they wear striped blue and white skirts, rings, necklaces and a switch with which they beat their brothers of circumcision. The knives have a red handle made from the skin of the red-headed agama lizard (*nankaryo*). Around their chests, they wear burial cloth and a large bag of arrows. In their hands they carry bows. All go to the crossroads and are fed millet rolled in raw sesame and smoked meat in sesame or salt sauce by the clown. The foot of a chicken is cut and touched on the bows, knives and heads of the clown and boys. The boys beat each other back to the village.

III Sticking of the bow: *taabfāakyo*

(a) The sticking of the bow is carried out after a man's death and before his skull-ceremony. It effectively releases his possessions and makes his wives available for remarriage to outsiders.

(b) The man's skull has hitherto been in a pot up a tree outside the village. His penis sheath, sleeping mat, knife, bow and quiver, hoe and clothes have been in the dead men's shelter beside the cattle-park.

(c) The clown, brother of circumcision and kinsmen of the dead man assemble in the dead men's shelter. His widow sits outside, hands in lap and must not move since this would make the rites difficult to perform. Two days earlier the clown blew his flute around the shelter while water was poured on the fermenting beer. This beer is now ready to drink. The clown fetches the skull of the dead man and his bow is cut off at both ends using the dead man's knife. A stone called *daatsumoh* 'ants' death-drum' and a piece of broken pot are attached at each end together with *fāazuulyo* 'head-sticker' and *fāanekyo*. They are tied with *yaahutu* and *bosohse* grass. Difficulty in executing this operation will be ascribed to adultery on the part of the widow. A similar group of three pieces of pot and the same leaves are tied to the middle of the bow. This is termed the 'navel'. The whole is drenched in red ochre and beer. The sorcerer or clown blows his flute. The 'navel' is cut also. Blood from a chicken's foot is touched on the bow and the clown's left shoulder.

(d) The men put on penis sheaths and blow the flute. All women flee. The men remove their clothes and seize part of the roof of the dead man's hut and his calabash. They rush off into the bush with the roof on fire and carrying the effects of the dead man. If the skull has not been brought to the village, they pick it up on the way and all run to the skull-house. The skull is placed outside, since its skull-festival has not yet been celebrated. The bow is attached behind. The clown or sorcerer announces: 'We have brought you your grandson.' The men sing the *yaako* circumcision song. The roof is pushed into the branches of a tree. The rest is buried under a tree at the place of circumcision.

(e) The act of circumcision is mimed. The brother of circumcision leans against a tree, the kinsman of the dead man holds him. The clown leaps out growling like a leopard and pretends to cut his penis. Sometimes a red thread is tied round it and the 'circumciser' removes this. The 'circumcised' crouches in the water of the river and the others splash him singing the *lore*. He ties grass round his penis and all put on *diiblyo* leaves. The men return to the village.

(f) The men perform 'the beating to death of the old Fulani woman' (see Appendix II (f) and chapter 6) in the public circle.

(g) A man slices up the *zohaale* yam and makes tracks with it round a tree. The others track it, fire an arrow into it, fire the arrow into the tree and break it off.

(h) They hang up their leaves and dress. The women reappear with beer. The men rub their hands with various pungent grasses. Beer is poured on the ground. Men and women touch it. All drink.

(i) This element may either precede or follow (h). The widows crouch in the dead man's compound while all his possessions are passed out by the sorcerer/clown, brothers of circumcision and kinsmen. The clown trims the widows' hair at the temples. The women and children of the dead man are sprayed, together with the goods, with water and germinated millet which the clown spits on them three times. The brothers of circumcision of the dead man each remove one thing that belonged to the dead.

(j) All go to the crossroads. The widow is wearing *gbungtyo* and *silkoh*. A piece of pot is dipped in oil and red ochre and placed on the head of the widow by the clown. He knocks it off into the bush. A brother of circumcision smears oil and ochre on her belly, a female relative does the same on her back. The widow puts on everyday leaves and lianas. She is fed smoked meat and salt or cooked sesame and given the star-shaped haircut. Three times she spits out the food, the fourth time she swallows. She dips a chicken's left foot in ochre and oil and touches it against the clown's forehead and left shoulder. She says to all present: 'If you give me something that's good. If you give me nothing that's good.'

IV Jar-ceremony: *rohtumyo* ('decoration')

(a) The jar-ceremony can be celebrated at any time after the death of a woman by her husband's people. It precedes her skull-ceremony. It may also be celebrated for a dead uncircumcised boy or an unmarried girl, but this will often be dispensed with.

(b) A water-jar of the dead woman is placed on a *helle* mat and surrounded by necklaces and iron bracelets. It spends the night here. It stands on a ring of *sole* grass and has *sole* wrapped around the neck. The brothers of the dead woman come from their village and drink beer round the jar. The heads of husband and daughter are shaved in the star-shape. The jar is full of *fonio* beer.

(c) The husband's *pabi* (SiDa) dresses in *tarko* leaves and sprinkles germinated flour into the pot with the left hand. 'Marie, come and take your beer.' The fermentation of the beer is taken as showing the presence of the spirit of the dead woman. It is considered important that the fermentation should be even. The woman's brothers call out her birth name. 'Come and take your millet, we are returning to our village.' The women of the village call out her married name and lick the jar 'to become pregnant'.

(d) The *wangbedo* flutes are blown. The women circle the jar singing Pape and Fulani songs. They are joined by the men. The women wave empty calabashes. The pot is half emptied and a woman washes it. The jar is taken by the brothers of the dead woman. A millet stalk is pushed into the neck and a red hat attached. A white robe, then a blue robe are added. 'Rain irons', broad hoe-blades, horsetails and sheep-skins are attached with burial cloth. Bracelets and necklaces are draped round it. Fermenting beer is spat on the jar and the belly of the daughter of the deceased by the dead woman's brothers. The left foot of a chicken is cut and rubbed on the foreheads of the dead woman's daughter, husband and the jar.

(e) The jar is carried out of the back of the compound. A young man dances with it. He is no particular class of relative. He wears bells attached to his ankles. The dance is that performed by decorated boys just before circumcision.

(f) The jar is taken to the crossroads and unwrapped. It is smeared with oil and red ochre. The brothers carry it off, half full of beer, to their village. In western Dowayoland, it must be kept in a hut without a beaten floor. In eastern Dowayoland, it is placed in the bush with the skulls of female ancestors.

(g) The husband and daughter are taken to the crossroads, decorated with bracelets, necklaces etc., smeared with oil and ochre, and are fed meat in cooked sesame or salt and millet rolled in raw sesame, by the clown.

V Burial: *workkpamsyo*

(a) Dowayos distinguish between the burial of a man, especially a rich man, and the burial of a woman. Uncircumcised males are buried as women. A man is transported to the dead men's shelter beside the cattle park. Only circumcised males may enter. The man is covered with oil and red ochre and dressed in a blue and white striped skirt. If he or his father was a killer, red *diiblyo* bark is placed in the mouth and on the elbows. His feet are bound, right over left, with *sole* grass and he is oriented with the head to the west. His brothers rush round the village blowing the *wangɓedo* flute. This will continue intermittently until the body is buried. The body lies on its back in a crouching position.

(b) A bull is selected. It must not be imperfect in body. If the dead man is the chief, the lead steer will be taken. Red ochre and oil are rubbed on its head and back. It is thrown on its back next to the corpse and its throat is cut. The skin is placed on the cadaver with its head on his head. The flesh may be eaten only by the circumcised. Only the clowns may eat the head.

(c) The men go out to the crossroads accompanied by clowns, sorcerers and brothers of circumcision of the dead man. Two clowns sit face to face at the crossroads. They prop up two pieces of grass over their heads. One says: 'Will you give me your cunt?' The other replies: 'You may have my cunt.' They simulate coitus with a stick. The grass is fired. They run shouting to join the other men. The men tie up a piece of termite hill with *diiblyo* bark. They make their way back to the village. Three times they stop, shout 'Yoh!' and beat the ground with sticks. They do this a fourth time in the public circle and return to the shelter. The termite hill is thrown away.

(d) The meat from the first bull is cut into strips and roasted directly on the fire. One clown holds a strip hanging from his teeth and the long *baarkyo* gong in his hand. Another holds the long rattle 'hoe handle' three times. They go to the public circle where all, men and women, perform the same dance. A fire is kept burning beside the body, near the head.

(e) The body is wrapped for the first time. It is sewn directly into the cattle-skin with *bosohse* grass. The head must not be covered with cattle-skin but with goat-skin. This beast, a black male goat called the *ōliisyo* ('naked goat'), is given by the brothers of the dead, killed by the brothers of circumcision and its excrement is rubbed on the body.

(f) Intermittent dancing continues for some three days. The widows may not enter their compounds but sit outside the dead men's shelter on long *gbohgle* mats. They will be taken to bathe every evening in the river by the dead man's sister. If it rains they may spend the night in the entry hut of their compound. They cannot cook. They are dressed in *silkoh* grass and *gbungtyo* leaves.

(g) The death-drum is placed before the *dore*. Whenever a relative arrives bearing burial cloth or skins, they circle the *dore* and the drum is beaten. Affines bring cloth and girls born in the village return. A man who has married a girl from the village ties his burial cloth round her belly. Wife-givers throw cloth at the faces of the dead man's kinsmen. The 'daughters of the village' brought back by their husbands put sheep-skins on their heads and dance. Their leader, the daughter of the dead man, receives a whole goat and wears a red hat. They dance to the *serereeyo*. They carry the woman in the red hat on their shoulders while dancing to the battle-song, then each daughter in turn.

(h) On the fourth day they wrap the body again. In former times, if a man had a herd of twenty cattle at least half would be killed. The government have forbidden this practice and nowadays only two or three will be killed and skinned. The meat is given to kinsmen, brothers-in-law receiving legs, or is sold. The skins will wrap the dead man.

(i) The corpse is wrapped in layers of burial cloth, followed by goat-skins, the whole assuming a pear shape. A white robe, then a blue, follow and more goat-skins and burial cloth are added. Finally cattle-skins are added and a red hat. A rich man will wear a *zuutaayo* feather on top. A fire is kept burning beside the body.

(j) The sons of the dead man dress up in the *sonyo* circumcision hat and wear burial cloth across their chests. Close relatives will wear *zepto* cactus to protect against the spirits of the dead.

(k) The brothers of circumcision go off and defecate together in the bush. The clown leads them back to the crossroads and shouts, beating on the ground with a millet stick. The sorcerer blows his flute. The women flee. They rush to the body and jostle it singing the *yaako* circumcision song. The sorcerer and a brother of circumcision drink beer made from the millet of the dead man. A brother of circumcision is carried to the public circle on the shoulders of another dancing man. They all sing the battle song. They dance back to the body each with his left hand on the shoulder of the man in front.

(l) In former times the body might well stay above ground for several weeks while dancing and feasting continued. Government interference has discouraged this and it is normally buried the next day. The men loop thongs of leather through the outer covering and drag it to a hole outside the village. As it leaves, a calabash is smashed against the bundle. It is buried vertically. Flat stones are used to cover the opening and a vertical stone is set in place. The tail is cut off the skin before burial and nailed to a *tarko* tree.

(m) The death of a female is different in several respects. A woman normally dies in her husband's village. She is normally wrapped there and then transported to her natal village where she is wrapped again. Burial is always in the natal village. This means that bodies are frequently being hauled considerable distances. If a woman dies in her natal village, kinsmen will often insist on carrying the body to the husband's village first, only to have to bring it back several days later.

(n) A woman is wrapped for the first time in her own compound by her brothers or other kinsmen. Women can be present. The body is tied, like a man's, and wrapped in any cattle-skin with a goat-skin over the face. Cattle may or may not be killed. The body is wrapped in burial cloth, goat-skin and cattle-skin. No blue or white robes are used.

(o) It is carried to the village of her father accompanied by the husband and sons dressed in *zompto* leaves and *silkoh* grass and playing *wangbedo* flutes. The women go out to receive the body banging empty calabashes and wailing. At the entrance to the village, there is a pause. The double gongs are beaten and the head of the compound appears in the gateway ringing a single bell. The body enters and circles the *dore* under which stands the death drum. This is beaten. The body is deposited in the public circle. The husband drinks beer and leaves blowing his flute.

(p) For poor men and women, the long tom-tom is not used, the *serereeyo* is not sung and the people do not carry each other on their shoulders. Instead, the women perform the *baatoh* where they scrape large calabashes back and forth across the ground and sing.

(q) Burial cloth and skins are brought by relatives and stacked in three groups before the *wagle*. The first is *dohdmihiiya* 'my own people', i.e. the natives of the village. The second is *waatnode* (MoBro's, i.e. wife-givers). The third is *fabinyo* (SiSo/Da, i.e. wife-takers).

(r) The body spends three days in the village. On the fourth day, the husband returns. He is met outside the village and shaved at the crossroads, together with his children. They put on *gbungtyo* leaves and *silkoh*. They carry calabashes from which they alone may eat. The men wear penis sheaths.

(s) The body is wrapped with goat-skins, burial cloth and cattle-skins for the last time. The women sing the *baatoh*. The men drink beer. Children of the woman sit on her belly. The husband kicks the body with his left foot: 'Well I'm leaving.' He must go without looking back.

(t) The body is buried in the same way as a man's.

(u) A special meal is prepared of the intestines of slaughtered cattle and sesame. Two male kinsmen of the deceased face each other across the death-drum and throw food at each other's faces. All relatives then eat the food. This is done for both male and female dead.

(v) The husband returns for the removal of the head some three weeks later. This is the same as for a man. Someone climbs into the grave and removes the skull from the now rotten corpse. It is cleaned with *tarko* leaves and examined for witchcraft. The presence of spikes behind the jaw indicates that the person concerned was a witch. If these are red or black, the witch has killed others. If they are broken off, the witch was killed by anti-witchcraft medicines. Molten grease is dripped on the skull. It is placed in a pot up a tree.

(w) About a month later, bereaved husband or wife can remove the *gbungtyo*. In the case of a dead man this is often collapsed together with the *taabfáakyo*, and I have described it as part of this festival (III (i) and (j)). For a man similar elements are involved when his wife dies. The belongings of the dead woman are piled in her compound and her sisters and the clown spit on both husband and goods. The man goes to the cross-roads and the clown shaves his head and rubs red ochre and oil on him. The sister gives him a white loincloth that he puts on and he flings away leaves and penis sheath. He is fed the smoked-meat meal.

Notes

1 The language should, correctly, be termed Doo[2]waa[23]yāa[1]yo[1], superscript figures indicating tone.

2 The archives at Poli variously group them with the Fali, Duru, Kirdi, Namchi or allude to them as a 'Teere' clan.

3 'Observation du Chef de région No. 97 le 6 avril 1939 au Chef de subdivision de Poli:
'L'évolution constatée chez les Namchis de l'Hosséré Nyoré au contact des Islamisés est à retenir. Que nous le veuillons ou non, cette attraction et cette influence des races supérieures sont de plus en plus sensibles sur les primitifs et c'est dans ce sens s'accomplissent [sic] les progrès constatés chez les populations au point de vue politique et social.

'Qu'un chef Kirdi ait tendance à jouer au petit lamido, à s'habiller de boubous au lieu de peaux de cabris, à posseder un cheval, une petite suite, ne nous doit point scandaliser. Il importe au contraire de favoriser cette évolution naturelle et d'en tirer profit pour mieux administrer les autotochtones chez lesquels l'anarchie est le principal obstacle que nous rencontrons.'

4 Note, for example, the many different notions of rationality that emerge from different participants in Wilson (1970).

5 The Dowayo term *namo* refers to the groups among whom the men are traditionally metalworkers and the women potters. I use the word *blacksmith* to include both men and women. Like many Dowayo terms this is prescriptive, i.e. a man is a blacksmith whether or not he exercises this occupation and there is nothing he can do about it.

6 See the court case described in Salasc (1943). Here a Dowayo blacksmith is charged with executing a sorcerer.

7 The Dowayo term is *nyēhse* 'root' used of all plant remedies whether or not the root is involved. It is used nowadays of Western drugs.

8 Some Dowayos use the term *namwagle* 'the *wagle* of wild beasts' but old men reject this as an incorrect and corrupt usage.

9 A Dowayo *yaako* circumcision song mocks circumcision candidates with the words:

Trembling, trembling,
You look as if you fear the knife,
Seize him, men!

I will cut him.
Cut him like a steer!
Cut him up like a buffalo!

10 For an earlier conception of this distinction, see Barley (1974). It is unfortunate that this reverses a strongly similar distinction made by Sapir (Sapir and Crocker 1977) but it is retained for reasons of consistency.

11 I am aware that this is a somewhat outmoded view of grammars as they are now written, but in this, as in other areas, anthropology can still use models that no longer command respect in the subjects where they originated. Thus the static models of the old structural linguistics underlie most of the cultural patterns perceived by anthropological structuralists.

12 Thus Fr. *aventure* becomes Ger. *Abenteuer* 'adventure' through association with Ger. *Abend* 'evening', i.e. 'a tale to be told in the evening'. The new form is no more nor less reasonable than the first but the change from arbitrary to motivated has been effected in part, still leaving, however, '*-teuer*' unmotivated.

13 For example, Trubetzkoy's (1949: 69–87) distinctions between bilateral, multilateral, proportional, isolated, privative, gradual and equipollent oppositions.

14 For example, on one occasion when men were removing the heads of the dead to examine them for witchcraft, they sent all the women away with the exclamation: 'If we bent down to retrieve a skull and farted would you tell no one?'
    Similarly, the gleeful coitus through stick and anus (Appendix V (c)) at burial is an assertion of the closure of the male body and the feminine nature of the anus.

15 This is something of an oversimplification. Both jars rest directly on *nyomptare* leaves on which rain-stones, cattle-stones, human skulls and the first grains of millet are placed.

16 This did not happen at every skull-festival I witnessed. Sometimes, there were three identical jars, one for women, one for uncircumcised and one for men. However, questioning showed that use of hearth and pierced jar were in the nature of optional embellishments that might or might not be used. For a full description of the rite see Appendix I.

17 See Appendix IV.

18 Boys and girls are named when they are first brought from the hut after birth. Subsequently, a boy changes his name at circumcision and a woman is normally given a new name by her husband. Changing of name is, however, not uncommon for reasons of personal taste and most Dowayos will have three or four names that they have used at one time or another. Chiefs are also known by the name of their village. Christians change names at baptism. Even small children indulge in the habit, and I have been gravely informed by children of

four or five that I must no longer call them by their old name as they have changed it.

19 Thus, cars have 'feet', 'eyes', 'ears' etc.

20 Appendix I (f), IV (c).

21 This provides an explanation for the observed high mortality amongst Dowayos who move to the cities and amongst boys after circumcision. One of the chief ordeals for suspected witches was to drink beer in which the knife of circumcision had been steeped overnight. Should the man be guilty, his belly would swell up with blood, and death or vomiting of blood would ensue.

22 A powerful specific is supplied by the thistle *guufyo* (*Leonitis repetifolia*) and the plant *nyomptare* (see note 15). The standard three powerful plants in Dowayoland are *zepto* (*Cissus quadrangularis*) a cactus, *geehlyo* (an odoriferous root) and *tule* (*Cyperus edulis*, a lily-plant with spiky leaves). These appear in many different types, all of which seem identical, and can only be distinguished by the circumstances in which they are efficacious. An interesting note on *zepto* and *tule* by an anonymous French colonial administrator of the 1940s is preserved in the archives at Poli and testifies to their similar use at that period.

23 The organiser of a skull-festival wears a hat decorated with porcupine quills and often *zepto* round his neck, as do close relatives at funerals.

24 Various other forms of *yaayo* exist, however, some of which are positively valued. They may bring such benefits as strong, clean teeth, success in cultivating or sexual good fortune. They are theoretically available against payment.

25 For methodological reasons, we should seek to pack as much information as possible into the structural description and so simplify the relevance restrictions as much as we can.

26 Other means of establishing innocence or guilt include plucking a stone from boiling water, leaping back and forth over a rope of *silkoh* to see if one becomes entangled, drinking beer laced with *dangoh* (*Euphorbia cameroonica*) poison and exposure to the knife of circumcision.

27 The Dowayo term *hin rahkyo* equates more or less with English 'saying' and may be either a literal or a metaphorical form.

28 In fact, of course, many other features are involved – hollowness, decoration, etc. Many rituals function to increase the strength of the equation by adding features, e.g. 'carried on shoulders', 'rubbed with oil' etc. As Black (1974) has pointed out, the main value and difficulty of metaphor derives from the indeterminacy of the posited similarities between given and hidden term.

29 In fact, as will be discussed later, there is some variation here from area to area. It was especially in the Mango and Daksidongo areas that the slaying of leopards was important. It is in the Mango area that the wearing of *zompto* for the first stage of mourning is quite generally replaced by *dalambo*.

30 *Yaahutu* has other names. It is also known as *yaatohutu, gbalóle, wadiwiilyo.* Their associations are darkness, nakedness, dirt. This material is thrown on dead bodies by skull-house sorcerers, attached to the bows of dead men, and the sorcerer's flute that can cause or cure blindness. A leopard-killer wears it around his waist. At the burial of a circumciser, his fellow-circumcisers wear skirts of it and he is buried covered in a pile of it. Given the role of excrement in relations with the dead, it seems clear that *yaahutu* is a form of vegetal excrement, manufactured as it is from bark that has been rotted under water.

31 This classification is widespread in Dowayo culture. The term suffixed by *-noyoh* is always the larger and more inclusive. Thus, *luknoyoh* 'old, female hut' is used by Dowayos to mean 'prison', *belnoyoh* is the more violent form of rain and *donnoyoh* is the largest form of jar. *-waatoh*, prefixed by the name of a plant, is the regular term for 'small branches of the plant' etc., while any element suffixed by *-walo* (male) is equivalent to 'small version of'.

32 I initially sought to establish the identification of the animal in this story with a lion and not an old female leopard by showing postcards with these animals portrayed on them. Old Dowayos, however, are unused to photographs and cannot recognise them – although their children can – and so I was reduced to buying pieces of skin, claws, etc. from the nearest 'Syndicat des guérisseurs traditionnels'. These were easily identified by old men and the case for the lion was unanimous.

33 It is a general theme of Dowayo disease etiology, that plants that cause disease (*zaase* 'pollution') cure it with remedies extracted from their roots (see note 7).

34 After writing this, I received a letter from my erstwhile assistant Matbo Matthieu describing a witchcraft-cleansing operation called *lelyáalikyo* 'crying on the place' which involves a sorcerer using a bull-roarer to emit the hunting call of a leopard.

35 Only the rounded *tiknoyoh* (or *daknoyoh*) – normally blackened on the inside – can be used to draw water. No other vessel may be placed in a spring or the source will become foul. Even a water-jar must be filled by placing the gourd in the water and emptying it into the jar.

36 Despite a long flirtation with the terminology of communication theory, anthropologists still often write as if predictability and meaning were the same thing. See especially Douglas (1975).

37 Thus, for example, the coin tossed to decide who will have choice of sides at the Boat Race. Any coin, provided it had two distinct sides, would do, but tradition demands that it be a sovereign of the year 1829 – the year in which the race was held for the first time.
   This is an interesting example in that it shows clearly the difference between the arbitrary signs of language systems and the ways in which symbolic systems outside language constantly try to shift from

the arbitrary to the motivated. It is only on Saussure's phonemic chessboard (1974: 22) that the nature of the pieces is irrelevant.

38 '... An uncircumcised boy has killed a fish in the bush ...' *Baatoh* song sung to mock a poor man at his funeral and express the unimportance of his death.

39 For a man *yaahutu* is added. Note that a millet stick is driven into the neck of the *rohtumyo* jar. Millet and *yaahutu* together are driven into the pile of first millet harvested by a 'true cultivator'.

40 For example, I was once fortunate enough to witness a discussion between Islamic northerners, Christian southerners and pagan montagnards. All agreed that the rainy climate at Ngaoundere was a good thing because it made their wives pregnant. The montagnards attributed this directly to the fact that it made their wives 'wet', the northerners said it was because the dry season left them more time for their wives who thus gave birth in the wet season. The southerners explained that the wet weather 'increased the vitamins' and thus led to greater fertility.

41 This is a standard motif in Dowayo symbolism. Ritual feeding is always by another person, usually the clown, e.g. Appendix I (j), II (i), III (j), etc. Rainchiefs, too, produce rain for all but may not drink it. The parallel with women is obvious since Levi-Strauss (1963). In Dowayoland, however, all cultural acts have this aspect of reciprocity. A man has to be decorated for circumcision by another, usually a SiHu, at death he must be wrapped by others, at the skull-festival carried by others. Possibly, this is to be viewed as part of the alien origin of culture that stems from the *Tarniisnohgbarklele* (see chapter 6).

42 This is perhaps the place to note that there is a plant called *kehllehse* 'scorpion food' which produces small red bulbous fruit. These are cooked and flung all round a compound on the occasion of (1) a girl's first menstruation and (2) the bringing to the village of the first millet of the year. The parallel between this and the throwing of porcupine excrement at Daksidongo skull-ceremonies to repel ancestors is clear. Remember that adultery also attracts scorpions. We can compare in fig. 39. If final brideprice payments have been made by the time of

wild animal food	digested	flung on skulls and skull-house	protects domesticated beasts and owners
wild plant food	cooked	flung on millet and village	protects domesticated fruits and owners
		flung on girl and village	protects domesticated sexuality and owners
		tied to penis	

Figure 39

onset of menstruation, the husband conducts the ceremony whereby the woman is shut up in the grinding house for three days. If payments have not been completed, the father conducts it in his compound. *Kehllehse* is attached to a boy's penis for re-entry to the village after circumcision.

43 To avoid confusion, I shall use the expression 'heads of millet' not in the English fashion to cover fruit and stalks, but in the Dowayo fashion where the 'head' is what is left when the seed has been extracted. The appropriate English term is then *hull* or *husk*.

44 Cockerels' eggs, as we should expect (see note 31), are smaller than hens' eggs and sterile. They are of great importance for the maintenance of fertility in several at least of the montagnard peoples.

45 This connects the rainstones with the human skulls which are similarly anointed (Appendix V (v)).

46 It is true that the Mango area takes its French name, *Vallée des rôniers*, from the fact that this is the only area of Dowayoland where such trees are abundant. However, *gbohgle* grass is abundant there too and borassus palms grow successfully where planted elsewhere in Dowayoland.

47 See note 39.

48 The sexual act itself is always a somewhat furtive, shuffling affair even between husband and wife. Neither party should be naked, clothing being simply pushed aside, and should be completed in total darkness. Contact with menstrual blood would be very dangerous to a man and render him catatonic. A woman must clean a man after intercourse to obviate this danger.

49 We should recall also (note 41 above) that a man's own millet only becomes accessible after millet of that year has been offered to him by another i.e. 'outside millet' precedes 'inside millet'. Similarly, a man's brothers' wives become accessible to him after their widowhood only after they have become available to outsiders.

50 The *taabmaatoh* is the name of a particular yam that grows in the dead men's shelter. It is of the species *zangyo*.

51 i.e. *zangyo* not *taabmaatoh*.

52 The rainpots are made by a (female) potter in the shelter. As far as I have been able to determine this is the only time that a woman ever enters.

53 That these are viewed as rules of culture not part of nature is evident from the Dowayo saying: 'The eyes do not avoid the mother-in-law's cunt.'

54 For example Gardi (1965). The whole of Gardi's description is vitiated by diffusionist assumptions and the unfortunate fact that he is apparently unaware that what he is witnessing is not the funeral of a typical Dowayo but the middle of the funeral of a circumciser with parts omitted owing to the conversion to Christianity of his eldest son.

55 Dowayos term this either *namkoohtyo* 'dried meat' or *namhõntilyo*.

The second element of this word is interesting. French-speaking Dowayos translate it, after some hesitation, as *viande pourrie* 'rotten meat'. It is also the word used for a potsherd.

56 The external motivation of the use of crossroads poses no great problem, in that they have point but no position and belong simultaneously to more than one track, i.e. are liminal space. Roads as a means of communication figure both in the agricultural rites at Daksidongo and in the case of the blacksmith who must leave the road and remain silent if he encounters threshed millet. The newly circumcised, who are controlled on the channels of food and speech, must build a bridge of *kurungkyo* leaves to cross a road and take it up after them.

57 The use of 'meaning' to refer to such information is an established and quite proper proceeding. The problem comes from the fact that language – whence the term is taken as totally unproblematic by anthropologists – can and does mean in many different ways that we seldom bother to distinguish (e.g. Leech 1975: chapter 1). The fact that human behaviour has communicative effect does not mean that it is a language, only that parts of it may be like parts of language. The fact that a woman is seen eating the smoked-meat meal at the crossroads does indeed communicate to a Dowayo that she is 'changing status' and links together all the various forms of this in his mind. This serves to motivate the usage by tying it to events with a perceived similarity.

But the meaning that we find here is the kind we find in language when a question: 'Have you seen my overcoat?' tells us that someone is about to leave. To suggest that the conceptual meaning of the sentence is 'I am about to leave' totally ignores a distinction between conceptual meaning and total communicative effect, without which linguistics could not even begin its task.

58 These are ideophones, outside the normal phonetic system of the language, and used especially for the linguistically difficult areas of taste, smell, types of motion, etc.

59 The actual point at which the blacksmith's part begins is subject to some variation.

60 There is even a rule that a blacksmith may not harvest his field at the same time that the field of a man who has died is being harvested.

61 Some skull-houses prescribe that the first millet of the year shall be placed, in a dry condition, on *nyomptare* leaves on the threshold of the hut. At Mango, moreover, it is at the skull-house itself that the first bush-fire of the year is lit.

62 This is also the name of the flute used by boys to 'talk' to women.

63 At this point, I introduce another ritual – 'the bringing out of the dogs' (*kaatuutigyo*). When dogs are old enough to be weaned and sold to others, the owner takes them in a basket to the crossroads, together with smoked meat, salt and sesame and millet on a broken pot. The dogs are fed, red ochre is mixed in the bowl and a red cross is made on it and on the dogs' foreheads and their owner's. A hole is pierced in

the dish and the millet stick used to stir the food is thrust through it to pin it to the ground. The dogs are driven back to the village. This stops them stealing, fouling the huts and wandering away. It is only after this point that dogs are named. We should note that boys lose their old names at circumcision just as ancestors do before being placed in the skull-house. It is only when the newly circumcised come back out of the skull-house that their new names are publicly announced.

64 If a woman wishes to take a husband from elsewhere, she may do so after being spat on at the 'sticking of the bow'. Then the yam remains permanently forbidden her (as do *sebure* and *sékoh* leaves that she would have worn).

65 The 'firecloth' *gbanlaayo* is claimed to be a captured Fulani battle-flag depicting red lizards (see above).

66 I understand that in some skull-houses the blue robe alone is used for funerals and the white robe alone for circumcision but I have not witnessed such a usage.

67 The sorcerer pronounces a curse if approached by a man whose property has been stolen and so communicates his *zaase* to the thief. Property may also be protected with *zaase* e.g. a blacksmith may attach part of a broken bellows to a tree whose fruit he wishes to reserve.

68 The circumciser has a remedy which should be spat on the belly and head of a pregnant woman to protect her from the 'hotness' of red and black monkeys that are particularly dangerous to small children. Originally this consisted of the skulls of these animals that were placed in a red and a black pot respectively. With time, the heads dissolved and the pots got broken, so now the remedy consists of a liquid with broken pot in it. There are clear chains of metaphoric and contiguous associations that motivate this practice externally but we are in an area here where internal motivation seems to resolve itself into the constant recombining of the same pot/head/stone/root elements.

69 Dowayos deny that it follows that one can tell whether or not a person is lucky by looking at their forehead. They explain that it is like the 'hot hands' of the hunter which feel no warmer than anyone else's.

70 Appendix I (i), III (c) (j), IV (d).

71 It is quite striking to an outsider how prescriptive are the categories of Dowayo life. On one occasion I asked a man where his *dōre* was and he led me to the cattle park and pointed to a spot on the ground. When I protested that there was nothing there, he confessed that the cattle had knocked it down but that was still the *dōre* as this was where it would be if he had one.

Bibliography

Ardener, E. 1970. 'Witchcraft, Economics and the Continuity of Belief', in *Witchcraft Accusations and Confessions*, Douglas, M. (ed.). London: Tavistock.

Arewa, E. and Dundes, A. 1964. 'Proverbs and the Ethnography of Speaking Folklore', *American Anthropologist* LXVI: 70–85.

Austin, J. 1962. *How to Do Things with Words*. Cambridge: Cambridge University Press.

Barley, N. 1974. 'Anthropological Aspects of Anglo-Saxon Symbolism', Unpubl. D.Phil. thesis. Oxon.

Barthes, R. 1967. *Elements of Semiology*. London: Cape.

Bateson, G. 1973. *Steps to an Ecology of Mind*. St Albans: Paladin.

Black, D. 1974. *Models and Metaphors*. Ithaca: Cornell University Press.

Cooper, D. 1974. *Presupposition*. The Hague: Mouton.

Douglas, M. 1975. *Implicit Meanings*. London: Routledge and Kegan Paul.

Dubois, J. *et al.* 1970. *Rhétorique générale*. Paris: Larousse.

Gardi, R. 1965. 'Über den Totenkult bei den Doayo in Nordkamerun', in *Festschrift Alfred Bühler*, Schmidt, C. (ed.). Basle: Pharos-Verlag.

Hays, D. 1970. 'Linguistic problems of denotation', in *Progress in Linguistics*, Bierwisch, M. and Heidolph, K. (eds.). The Hague: Mouton.

Jakobson, R. 1966. *Selected Writings*, vol. IV. The Hague: Mouton.

Katz, J. and Fodor, J. 1963. 'The Structure of a Semantic Theory', *Language* 39: 170–210.

Leach, E. 1964. 'Anthropological Aspects of Language: Animal Categories and Verbal Abuse', in *New Directions in the Study of Language*, Lenneberg, E. (ed.). Cambridge, Mass.: MIT Press.

Leech, G. 1975. *Semantics*. Harmondsworth: Penguin.

Lembezat, B. 1961. 'Les populations païennes du Nord-Cameroun et de l'Adamoua', in *Ethnographic Survey of Africa*. Vendome: Presses Universitaires de France.

Levi-Strauss, C. 1964. *Totemism*. London: Merlin.

Levi-Strauss, C. 1970. *The Raw and the Cooked*. London: Cape.

Llewellyn, K. and Hoebel, E. 1941. *The Cheyenne Way: Conflict and Case Law in Primitive Jurisprudence*. Norman: Oklahoma University Press.

McLeod, M. 1972. 'Review Article', *Social Anthropology and Language*, Ardener, E. (ed.). ASA 10. London: Tavistock.

Mauss, M. 1972. *A General Theory of Magic*. London: Routledge and Kegan Paul.

Needham, R. 1962. *Structure and Sentiment*. Chicago: Chicago University Press.

Salasc, L. 1943. 'Une ordalie en pays namchi', *Bulletin de la Société d'Etudes Camerounaises* 3.

Sapir, J. and Crocker, J. (eds.) 1977. *The Social Use of Metaphor*. Philadelphia: University of Pennsylvania Press.

Saussure, F. de. 1974. *Course of General Linguistics*. London: Fontana.

Skorupski, J. 1976. *Symbol and Theory*. Cambridge: Cambridge University Press.

Sperber, D. 1974. *Rethinking Symbolism*. Cambridge: Cambridge University Press.

Tambiah, S. 1968. 'The Magical Power of Words', *Man* 3, 2: 175–208.

Tambiah, S. 1969. 'Animals are good to think and good to prohibit', *Ethnology* 7: 423–59.

Tambiah, S. 1973. 'Form and Meaning of Magical Acts', in *Modes of Thought*, Horton, R. and Finnegan, R. (eds.). London: Faber and Faber.

Trubetzkoy, N. 1949. *Principes de phonologie*. Paris: Klincksiek.

Turner, V. 1967. *The Forest of Symbols*. Ithaca: Cornell University Press.

Wilson, B. (ed.) 1970. *Rationality*. Oxford: Oxford University Press.

Zamora, M. 1971. *Themes in Culture*. Phoenix: Alemar.

Index